What
Employers
Want

The employability skills handbook

Karen Holmes

2nd edition

trotman | t

What Employers Want: The employability skills handbook

This second edition published in 2017 by Trotman Education, an imprint of Crimson Publishing Ltd, 19–21c Charles Street, Bath, BA1 1AU.

© Karen Holmes 2017

British Library Cataloguing in Publication Data
A catalogue record for this book is available from the British Library.

ISBN: 978 1 91106 752 8

Typeset by IDSUK (Data Connection Ltd)
Printed and bound in Malta by Gutenberg Press Ltd

Contents

About the author

Karen Holmes is a freelance writer specialising in education, management and training. She has written a number of careers books as well as articles for magazines and journals on career development. She is the author of *Real Life Guide: Creative Industries*, *Careers Uncovered: Teaching* and *Careers Uncovered: Design*, all published by Trotman.

Acknowledgements

The second edition of this book has been a pleasure to write as it brought me into contact with so many inspiring young people who are setting out on their first careers. Motivated, enthusiastic and multi-talented, they are eager to join the world of work and willing to rise to the challenges they face. Thank you to all those who shared their aspirations and stories.

Many thanks also to the employers who talked honestly about what they really want from their teams. The information they provided about the job market in these times of rapid social and economic change was invaluable. It's good to see that so many of them are keen to offer opportunities to young people in their organisations.

Thank you to everyone who contributed. Thanks also to Della Oliver for being a sympathetic and helpful project manager and to all the team at Trotman for their support.

Introduction

About this book

Moving from school or college into work is one of the biggest steps you'll ever take. It's an exciting time but it's also a challenging one. Having spent most of your life in education – where you *have* to be whether or not you can think of better things to do – suddenly you're fighting to be accepted by an employer. And you're in competition with a lot of other people who are also trying to take that first step on the career ladder.

When newspapers publish headlines like 'Youth unemployment rate is worst for 20 years' (*The Guardian*, 22 February 2015) and point out that the number of people aged 16–24 who are not in full-time education or employment has increased to 498,000, an unemployment rate of 14.4%, it's easy to feel that the world is against you before you start. However, it is important that you bear this point in mind: there are jobs out there if you are willing to seek them out. You may have to broaden your search and look at careers in disciplines you hadn't previously thought of; you may have to start at the very bottom of an organisation; you certainly won't earn megabucks – but you will find a job if you really want to.

One of the most important aspects of applying for a job is making an impression on employers by showing them what you can already do. You need to demonstrate your abilities when you complete an application form and go for interview – and you can't do that unless you know what your skills and abilities are. And once you start work, you need to be confident that you can fulfil your boss's expectations.

Many of us don't recognise what we're capable of because we've never really thought about it. At school or college we communicate with lots of different people, solve problems, make decisions and work in teams on a daily basis – but we don't equate this with the skills that employers ask for. So, when we see a job advertisement that asks for 'excellent communication, teamworking and problem-solving skills', we don't bother to apply because we think that we're under-qualified.

The purpose of this book is to help you recognise *what you can already do* and how you can transfer your abilities to a workplace where they are needed. With a little help, you can improve on these skills – and you can learn how to present them to potential bosses in a positive way.

This isn't another book about applying for jobs, filling in forms, writing CVs or going to interviews. Its focus is on helping you to identify and improve your skills, attitudes and behaviours so that you have the confidence to go out and show employers just how capable you are.

You can access and download some of the activities in this book by visiting trotman.co.uk/wew. This means you can complete them in detail and amend them as many times as you want as your skillset improves.

Who is this book for?

This book is for anyone who is looking for a job or about to start work. It will also help you if you're going into further/higher education and you want to know more about presenting yourself positively to colleges and universities.

What's this book about?

It's about you! We believe that you already have a lot of skills and abilities that will be helpful when you start work and that will make you a really useful member of an organisation. Unfortunately, many of you might not recognise just how capable you are because you don't translate what you do in everyday life into what employers ask for.

What do we mean by skills?

'Employability skills' is a term that gets bandied around a lot, sometimes inaccurately. In this book we are focusing on the skills that the UK Commission for Employment and Skills (UKCES) have listed in their report *The Employability Challenge* as almost everyone needing to do in almost any job. These combine functional skills (such as being able to use numbers and IT effectively) and personal skills (like working together and communicating). These skills are combined with attitudes, values and habits (the way that you think and behave to define the sort of person that employers really value. You'll look at this subject in a lot more detail in Chapter 3. This publication contains public sector information licensed under the Open Government Licence v3.0.

How can this book help you?

This book will help you in many different ways to:

- recognise the skills that you already have and what you can already do
- understand how your existing skills will be useful when you look for a job or start work
- build on those skills, so that you become the sort of person that an organisation wants to employ.

Here's an example

Smith and Jones is a company of solicitors in a small market town. They want to employ a new office junior, somebody they can train up to become an office administrator. The partners at Smith and Jones have a meeting and draw up a list of skills, qualifications and qualities that their ideal applicant would have. Here are the things that they're looking for:

- a minimum of five GCSEs, including English and maths at grades A*–C
- familiarity with Microsoft software, including databases and spreadsheets
- good communication skills so that the new staff member can interact with lots of different people, from senior partners to clients
- a team player: someone who pulls their weight and can work happily with everyone else in the company
- problem-solving skills: someone who can think in a logical way and work out an answer to a problem
- organisational skills: the job will involve a lot of sorting, filing and tidying!
- a willingness to study for qualifications that relate to the job.

Gemma is 17 years old and studying for her A levels in ICT, psychology and sociology. She's already decided that she doesn't want to go to university but would like to find a job that will give her some sort of training and offer her a future. She's quite enjoyed school – she's good at sport and has captained the netball team for two years. For the past 12 months she's had a weekend job helping out as a volunteer in a charity shop and she loves the work, helping to sort through the donations and display the stock. Although she's fairly shy, she gets on well with the other staff and they know they can rely on her to get a job done. The customers like her too, because she takes the time to listen to them and get to know them. In her spare time, Gemma helps out at home by looking after her brothers and sisters when her parents are working. They have a small business and she occasionally helps them with the accounts – nothing complicated, but she can use spreadsheets, which is more than her dad can do!

Gemma learns about the vacancy at Smith and Jones. This is the sort of job that she'd like; it sounds interesting and would give her a chance to develop a real career in administration – plus the law interests her as it's featured strongly in her sociology and psychology courses. She sends off for an application form but, after reading the list of qualities that the company is looking for, she decides that it's not worth applying. What's the point? She's got the right GCSEs and she's good with computers but communication, teamwork, problem-solving and organisational skills – she's not been trained in these. She believes that she hasn't got a hope of getting an interview.

That's sad, because Gemma is a good candidate for this job. She has the skills that the employer needs – she just doesn't recognise them.

- She's already working successfully in a job where she deals with the public – which suggests that her communication skills are well developed.
- She's captained the netball team – not only is she a team player in every sense of the word, but she can organise and give instructions when necessary.
- She helps her parents at home and in their business – so she's already developed a lot of organisational and problem-solving skills.

Her studies are relevant to Smith and Jones's work. The sociology course included work on crime and deviance; the psychology course underpins her knowledge and understanding of human behaviour – including factors that can lead to people experiencing problems in their lives that might need resolving by the law; her ICT course involves a range of practical skills from programming through to managing cyber-security, all of which give her a good academic background for the specified job.

She's also keen to build a career so would be happy to take on studies related to professional qualifications if the chance arose.

If Gemma could look at herself objectively and work out exactly what skills she already has, she would recognise that she has a good chance of getting the job. Her problem is not lack of *ability* but lack of *confidence* and *self-knowledge*.

This book will help people like Gemma by encouraging them to relate what they can already do to what employers want when they are looking

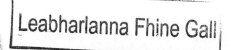

for staff. If you're in a similar position to Gemma – or if for any reason you want to weigh up just who you are and how good you are – then this book will:

- encourage you to carry out a personal skills analysis
- highlight what skills you need to develop or acquire
- build on your existing skills so that you can make a genuine contribution at work
- help you to create a skills profile that you can use when you apply for jobs.

This book isn't just for job-seekers. Many of the skills that employers want are also useful when you go into higher education. At university or college, you'll need to build up your communication, organisational, problem-solving and teamworking skills. If you're intending to continue your education, it will help you to present yourself more effectively when you go for interviews and to settle into academic life.

Raising the participation age

As you're probably aware, young people now have to stay in education or training until they are 18 years old. You have the following options:

- Study full-time at school, college or with a training provider. Further study has become increasingly important in helping young people meet employers' skills requirements and compete in the job market.
- Work or volunteer full-time (full-time is counted as more than 20 hours a week) combined with part-time study or training. You must have a job that offers training.
- Take up an apprenticeship. The government is committed to increasing the number of apprenticeships to 3 million by 2020.

All these pathways have one thing in common: until you are 18, whether you are in employment or still at school, you must find a way to improve your skills and learning. Consequently, the emphasis on employability skills has never been higher.

What's in this book?

Chapter 1: What skills do you need to succeed at work?

In this chapter, we look at the different types of skills, attitudes and behaviours that this book explores and examine why they're so important in the workplace. In particular, we look at how improving your *functional* skills (using numbers, language and ICT) and your *personal* skills (self-management, problem solving, teamworking and communicating) can help you to get the job you want, or improve your performance if you're going into higher education.

Chapter 2: Where are you now?

Here we focus on you and what you've already achieved. Where are you now in terms of the skills, attitudes and behaviours you already possess? We'll help you to carry out a skills analysis so that you recognise the skills that you already use, both in school and socially. There are new sections in this chapter that highlight the importance of the way that you think; as well as looking for the functional and personal skills we identified in Chapter 1, employers also seek determination, optimism and emotional intelligence in their staff.

Chapter 3: Where do you need to be?

When you've identified what you can do now, you need to think about where you need to get to in order to find a career that you'll enjoy. This chapter looks at the skills, attitudes and characteristics that employers look for and the language they use when they ask for them. We'll help you to decode job adverts so that you have a clearer understanding of what recruiters are looking for. Then we'll help you to draw up an action plan so that you can build on your existing skills.

Chapter 4: Using numbers effectively

This chapter explores one of the most important functional skills that employers look for: the ability to use numbers effectively. Maths may not have been your favourite subject at school, but competence in using numbers in different situations is a huge bonus when you're working. We examine why using numbers accurately is important in the workplace and highlight the areas of work where it is relevant, from simple budgeting and calculating wages and accounts, through to working out dimensions, space and angles.

Chapter 5: Using language effectively

Almost every job advertisement that you look at will ask for 'communication skills' – but what exactly does this mean? In this chapter we'll explain some of the principles of using language precisely so that your meaning is always clear. In particular we'll look at written communication. Later, in Chapter 9, you'll look at teamworking and communication where you'll explore listening, speaking and interpreting body language. In a new section, we'll explore using digital communication and social media in the workplace – and how it differs from the way you use it with your friends!

Chapter 6: Using ICT effectively

Almost every workplace uses ICT in some form or other, so most employers like their staff to be comfortable with computers and other electronic and digital systems. This chapter examines ICT in the workplace and outlines some of the tasks that you might be asked to do, such as using spreadsheets and preparing presentations.

Chapter 7: Self-management

When you start work, you'll have to take on a lot of responsibility not only in your work but also in managing yourself. How should you present yourself through your dress and your manner to impress your colleagues? How will you manage to turn up for work on time every day? In this chapter we look at why this is important and how you can improve your self-management skills. We also consider how you can learn to ask for help to overcome any challenges you face. When you start work, you'll find that you continually need to upgrade your skills. We look at why this is so important in the workplace and how you can take charge of your own learning. We'll help you to assess your skills on an ongoing basis and identify areas where you need to improve. Then we'll suggest ways in which you can get additional help and training if you need it.

Chapter 8: Thinking and solving problems

How do you solve problems and make decisions? Do you trust your instincts and then hope for the best? We're going to look at more systematic approaches to problem solving and explain why these can help you to make better decisions. In this chapter you'll look at a number of techniques that you'll find useful in any situation – at work, school or at home – where you have to solve a problem or make a decision.

Chapter 9: Working together and communicating

Why is working in teams or groups so popular and what benefits does it bring to individuals and organisations? In this chapter you'll find out as you explore how a team develops, what roles different members of a team can play and how you can work more effectively within your own team. You'll also continue looking at communication – something you started in Chapter 5. Here you'll focus on speaking, listening and body language and we'll give you some tips to improve your competence.

Chapter 10: Understanding the business

Nobody works in a bubble. What you do impacts on your colleagues, the managers and company owners and your customers. In this new section, we explore why it's important to look at the big picture and to learn as much as you can about the organisation you work for. How does your job fit into the whole? Where do you fit into the business? What are stakeholders and how do they influence what you do at work? And, when you understand the business you're in, how can you contribute to it?

Chapter 11: Write your own profile

In this chapter, you'll review what you've achieved as you worked through this book. You can then prepare a skills profile that identifies what you can already do and, most importantly, gives evidence of your skills. You can use this as a basis for job or higher education applications and refer to it before interviews. When you're feeling a bit unsure of your future, it will give you confidence by providing a permanent record of how many skills you already possess.

Chapter 12: Further information

This chapter contains a list of further contacts – organisations that can help you to continue developing your employability skills. We've included a brief glossary that offers definitions of terms that might be unfamiliar to you.

We're not going to pretend that this book will guarantee you a job – nobody can do that! However it will help you to evaluate just how capable you are and to build on your skills and abilities. That should improve your self-confidence so that you feel better equipped to apply for the jobs you're interested in. After that – it's up to you ...

Good luck!

1 What skills do you need to succeed at work?

This chapter introduces you to the concept of skills and, in particular, employability skills that are so important when you start work. Later in the book, you'll explore each of the skills areas in greater depth, but first let's consider what particular aptitudes and abilities we're talking about and why they're so important.

Employability skills

'Employability skills' is a term that we hear a lot. So what does it actually mean?

The UK Commission for Employment and Skills (UKCES) defines employability skills as 'the skills almost everyone needs to do almost any job'. This extract from the Skills for Life Network website (www.skillsforlifenetwork.com) explains:

> Employability skills build up in three layers, starting with a foundation of Positive Approach, which includes: being ready to participate, making suggestions, accepting new ideas and constructive criticism and taking responsibility for outcomes.
>
> This base of Positive Approach supports the three functional skills of using numbers, language and ICT effectively. These functional skills are utilised in the context of four personal skills:

What Employers Want

- self-management
- thinking and solving problems
- working together and communicating
- understanding the business.

Employability skills therefore combine three factors.

1. Your attitude towards work – you have to want to do the job to the best of your ability. This positive attitude will underpin everything you do at work – it's what makes you a good employee.
2. Your literacy, numeracy and ICT skills, which support your performance at work. Whatever job you get, these skills will help you to work confidently and acquire the knowledge you need to carry out your job.
3. Your personal skills – your ability to manage yourself so that you fit in with the demands of the job and the organisation you work for.

Let's look at an example.

You are set on becoming an electrician and want an apprenticeship. When you are interviewed by a potential employer, they are looking for enthusiasm and a 'can do' approach. The candidate who stands out will be someone who is genuinely seeking an apprenticeship and isn't just going through the motions because they can't think of anything else to do.

The employer will want to know about your ability to learn. Your apprenticeship will involve lots of training and learning; will you be up to that? One way of assessing your potential is to examine your functional skills – how well you use language, numbers and ICT. These skills form the foundation of your future learning.

Finally, the employer will assess how well you'll fit into the organisation by examining your personal skills. Are you reliable, punctual, polite, smart? When you face a problem do you look for a solution or burst into tears? Do you try to get on with people or do you expect them to make all the effort?

These are the qualities that most employers look for.

Why are employability skills so important?

Employability skills have become increasingly important because the way that we structure our careers has changed so dramatically. If you had been born 50 years ago you would probably have:

- finished school at 15 years old and trained for a job, or
- stayed on at school until you were 18 years old, gone to university and then trained for a job
- continued to work in the same profession or trade for the rest of your life
- probably worked for the same employer, in the same place, for much of that time.

During that time you might have acquired new skills, and your job may have developed and changed in some ways, but essentially you would have done the same work.

Today, the average length of time people spend in one job has shortened dramatically to less than five years! We live in an age when employees feel free to change employers in order to get promotion, earn more money, move to another area, find more interesting work ... There is no longer pressure to stay with a company if it does not give you what you want.

There has also been a rise in what are known as 'portfolio careers' where individuals have a series of short-lived jobs, or two or three part-time jobs at the same time, in order to build up experience and widen their contacts.

The employment market – and the way that we think about work – has changed almost beyond recognition. Staff no longer mark the success of their careers by length of service but by how quickly they move up the career ladder. People are recruited and promoted on merit, not according to how long they've been with the company.

All this mobility means that employability skills have become a lot more important. It is expensive for employers to train up staff from scratch so they want recruits who have some proven skills that are useful in the workplace. Yes, they may be willing to train you to carry out particular parts of your new job – but they like to know that you already have a good command of the personal skills that you need in the workplace and that you have a positive attitude towards work.

For young people who are just starting work, this can be very daunting. You know that you can do many things well but you've not had a chance to prove yourself. You don't have anything much to put on your CV that looks impressive. And, to make matters worse, you keep hearing that employers are unhappy because the standard of young job applicants is so poor ...

The problem for employers

In 2015, the Chartered Institute of Management Accountants polled 1,700 of its members and found that a third (31%) of firms took more than two months to fill junior posts and when they did most of the new recruits (75%) needed significant training.

It also found that:

- more than 90% of firms reported that their workload had increased as a result of skills shortages
- UK candidates were twice as likely to lack functional skills, basic literary and numeracy, than their European peers
- 46% of finance bosses agreed that the lack of skill of junior employees has significantly impacted on performance
- 40% of UK firms felt candidates lacked essential skills, compared with less than a fifth (18%) of those on the Continent.

It's not just accountants who are having problems finding suitable young staff. Their complaints echo across many other industries.

In this book we're looking at the functional and personal skills employers want you to have and also the attitudes that need to underpin everything you do.

Positive approach

Getting a job, and succeeding in that job, depend on many different things. One of the most important is your attitude. You must be willing to work, open to new experiences, able to take instructions and to learn. You need to be ready to participate in all aspects of the business, make suggestions and accept responsibility. You must be able to deal positively with criticism and learn from it without getting upset or angry.

Primark is a giant fashion retailer with more than 57,000 employees. This extract gives a flavour of what they look for in their staff.

> The people who work for us in our stores need to reflect the company's culture and values. They need to be bright, enthusiastic and always helpful – to customers and other members of their team. And they must want to keep improving the way that they and Primark work.

Even more informative is a section on the website that coaches applicants about the Primark interview process. This really sets out the qualities that are important to the company.

> You can practise before you come for your interview by thinking of specific examples where you have been challenged or demonstrated a certain skill. This will give you an idea of what to use as examples to the questions.
>
> Here are a few things to consider:
>
> ▪ Passion and motivation
> ▪ Communication skills

- What interests you about the position?
- Career aspirations – what is your goal?
- Organisational and prioritising ability
- Honesty and reliability
- Business awareness/ company knowledge
- Pro-activity rather than reactivity

Source: www.primark.com/en/careers/careers-at-primark/retail-sales-team.

Think about it: there are probably areas in your life where you already display these qualities. Now you need to transfer them to work.

Functional skills: Using number, ICT and language effectively

There are very few jobs that don't require you to use numbers and ICT in some way, so it's easy to see why these functional skills are so important. It's basic ability that's important, not your knowledge of quadratic equations or your speed at programming a computer.

What an employer is looking for is a positive approach. They want to know that you won't run for the hills if you're asked to do some simple calculations and that you will approach a task willingly. They want to know that the sight of a computer doesn't reduce you to tears. You can be trained in the particular numeracy and ICT skills that relate to your job but you have to be open to that training and happy to do it – and that won't happen if numbers and ICT frighten you.

Using language accurately is another essential functional skill. More problems in life are caused by poor communication than by anything else. Think about it; if you've ever played the game Chinese Whispers, where a message is passed in whispers around a circle of people, you'll know how quickly it can get distorted. 'Send reinforcements, we're going to advance' becomes 'Send three and four pence, we're going to a dance!'

Similarly, problems can arise when individuals find it difficult to communicate effectively in writing. A badly written report, a misspelled letter to a customer, an email that is so badly punctuated that it doesn't make sense: all of these can adversely affect a business.

Think about miscommunication in the context of your school or college life. How many times have you struggled with a piece of work because of one of the following?

- You didn't listen to the instructions – you were daydreaming.
- You listened to the instructions but they were so garbled that you didn't understand them.
- You listened to the instructions and understood them but you were distracted by someone else and forgot what you'd been told to do.

Essentially, language and communication skills are about getting a message from one person to another clearly and unambiguously. This involves five different abilities.

4. The ability to *speak clearly* so that others understand your message.
5. The ability to *listen properly* so that you hear and understand what other people are saying to you.
6. The ability to *write clearly* so that other people can read your message and understand it.
7. The ability to *use correct grammar and spelling*.
8. The ability to *interpret other elements* that contribute to communication, such as body language and other 'non-verbal signals'.

Getting a bad result in your schoolwork because of poor communication may be distressing; doing something wrong at work because of poor communication can be dangerous.

When you start work, you'll use your language and communication skills all the time to:

- tell people what to do
- receive instructions
- make friends and generally 'get along' with people
- understand the bigger picture about what is happening in your organisation.

It's hardly surprising, then, that employers like to find recruits who already have a firm grasp of basic communications skills on which they can build.

Personal skills: Self-management

Self-management means just what it says: the ability to monitor and improve your behaviour so that it complies with what your job demands. This includes areas such as setting goals and managing your time. As we've said before, when you start work you'll get much less supervision than you did in school or college; it will be up to you to demonstrate responsibility and reliability. That means managing your behaviour so that you fulfil your employer's needs.

Personal skills: Thinking and solving problems

Every minute of every day, we use our thinking skills to solve problems and make decisions. We use our creativity to come up with solutions about everything from how to write an essay to what clothes to wear. We reflect on what we have done and learn from our actions. (If I hadn't got up late this morning, I wouldn't have rushed downstairs this morning, tripped on the stairs and hurt my ankle. Tomorrow I'll get up earlier!) We analyse situations and develop solutions. (Now that I've got a bad ankle I can't drive so I have to work out another way to get the groceries I need.)

Much of the time, we don't even realise that we're doing it. Using a blend of experience, knowledge, instinct and guesswork we come up with answers and decide what to do. The problem is that using this combination of techniques doesn't always give us the right solution. As with language and communication skills, getting the wrong answer isn't always that serious. When you're at work, however, it can have repercussions that affect both you and your employer.

There are no strict rules to thinking and problem solving effectively, but you can learn techniques that help you to work through the evidence, balance up the options and come up with the best solution for the circumstances in which you are operating. By learning these techniques and enhancing your problem-solving skills, you'll make fewer mistakes.

In a work context, this is important. Look at what shop manager Martina has to say.

When I started work as a retail assistant, there was always someone more experienced to turn to if I had a problem with a customer or the equipment in the shop. Now that I'm managing one of our branches, it's up to me to come up with solutions. It's not always easy because every day there are issues to deal with: stock hasn't arrived, there's an electricity cut and we have no power for the tills, a customer is trying to return goods that have been used.

In many cases, we have policies to deal with these problems so I know what to do, but you can't have an answer prepared for every situation and sometimes it's up to me to make the decision about what to do. Also, I'm involved in making decisions that have an impact on how well our shop performs. I'm the one who tells head office what stock will sell and who has to come up with a plan to increase sales during a slack period. I've had to become a lot more systematic and logical about the way in which I approach problems systematically; I weigh up the evidence and think about the impact that my decisions will have rather than act on impulse. Most importantly, I've learned to be more consistent – I can't just change my mind on a whim because it affects so many other people.

Martina says that her friends used to describe her as impetuous, and more inclined to speak and do than spend a lot of time thinking. She's had to acquire a lot of new problem-solving and decision-making skills because she can't afford to make mistakes.

> Luckily my employers invest heavily in training and they've spent a lot of time making sure that I'm equipped to deal with the situations that I face at work. I've worked with more experienced staff and at head office to learn more about our organisation's way of thinking and this has influenced the way that I think about the problems that arise.

Interestingly, this approach has had an effect on other parts of her life.

> I'm much less inclined to fly off the handle or make a snap decision at home than I used to be and I think everyone has benefited from that!

Many people find themselves in the same situation as Martina: the more their career develops, the more responsibility they have to take for problem solving and decision making. Consistency is important – making sure that every problem and every person is dealt with in the same way – and this can only be achieved if problems are dealt with systematically and the solutions applied with an even hand. Martina has changed her approach and learned new skills in order to deal with the changes in her working life.

Personal skills: Working together and communicating

Very few jobs ask you to work in isolation and increasingly businesses organise their operations using different teams to carry out different tasks. Groups of people are asked to join forces and work cooperatively. This has the advantage of pooling resources; if you have a team of people you will generally have access to a wider range of skills and abilities than if you rely on one person.

Some people believe that being able to work in a team is a talent that you're born with rather than a skill that you can learn. You've probably come across individuals who say that they are 'loners', who don't like being part of a group and do their best to wreck any teams that they're part of.

In fact, anyone can be an effective team worker if they choose to be. Obviously, it helps if you want the team to succeed but even the most committed 'loner' can make a contribution if they develop their team-working skills. Teamworking demands that you can both co-operate with others and be assertive if the situation demands it. You need communication skills so that you can speak clearly to a wide range of people and listen to their response, persuade them if necessary, and keep them on track.

These skills involve understanding the dynamics of a team, and accepting that teams work because they're made up of different types of people. Just because someone is very different from you doesn't mean that you can't work with them. The blend of diverse personalities can make a team effective – providing that the team members know how to manage their behaviour so that everyone plays their part.

Personal skills: Understanding the business

When you start work, you'll be part of an organisation. It may be a multi-million-pound global corporation such as a bank that employs thousands of people; it could be a small family-run consultancy that only has a handful of staff. Nevertheless, it is an organisation in which different people will have different responsibilities and into which you will have to find your place.

The more you learn about the company with which you wish to work – its products/services, structure, what it believes in, where it wants to go in future – the bigger your advantage when it comes to getting a job. Being aware of the environment that the company works in shows that you have a genuine interest in the employer and have done your homework.

Understanding the business will also help you to decide if an employer is right for you – and that can save you a lot of time and heartache in the long run. An interesting development since the first edition of this book came out is the number of recruitment websites for organisations that show interviews with staff who describe their work and lives. If they interest you, you're applying to the right place; if your reaction is negative and you can't bear the thought of working with these people in the environment they are describing – look elsewhere for a job!

In the next chapter, we're going to focus on *you* to help you assess what skills you've already mastered that could be useful to an employer.

Get ready to answer some questions!

2 Where are you now?

You want a job. Employers want to find staff for their organisations. Why, then, do we read so many articles about individuals struggling to find work? Why are a lot of young people 'unemployable'?

The government and various industrial and professional organisations have carried out a lot of research into 'employability' skills in an attempt to find out what skills, qualities and attitudes make young people suitable for work.

As we've seen in the first chapter, the UK Commission for Employment and Skills has set out a list of skills that almost everyone needs to do almost any job. In their publication *First Steps: A New Approach for Our Schools*, the Confederation for British Industry (CBI) identified a list of 'characteristics, values and habits that last a lifetime' that they believe are essential for people to succeed in employment, included below. These are very much personal qualities and include determination, optimism and emotional intelligence.

The list is quite precise in what it states young employees should exhibit in their behaviour and attitudes. Don't be put off by this; most of the qualities they identify are ones that you probably already have!

You should be determined

That means you should exhibit grit, resilience, tenacity. In practical terms this means:

- understanding the value of work not just in financial terms but how important it is to our sense of self-worth
- finishing tasks you've started and not giving up when the going gets rough
- learning to take positives from any failure you experience; we can learn a lot from our mistakes and use that learning to create success.
- working independently and focusing on solutions
- exhibiting self-control by paying attention and resisting distractions – when you're at work, you're at work and that's what you focus on
- remembering and following directions
- starting work right away rather than putting it off – put that phone away!
- remaining calm even when you're criticised
- allowing others to speak without interruption
- being curious, eager to explore new things and to ask and answer questions to deepen your understanding.

You should be optimistic

That means you should exhibit enthusiasm, gratitude, confidence, ambition and creativity by:

- actively participating at work – volunteering, getting stuck in and not always waiting to be told what to do
- helping others to feel enthusiastic about their work, not moaning or being grumpy
- appreciating the people you work with
- appreciating the opportunities you're getting at work
- being willing to try new experiences and meet new people
- being confident and ambitious – having goals that you want to pursue
- thinking creatively, identifying and developing new ideas.

You should have emotional intelligence

This means you should exhibit humility, respect and good manners, and sensitivity to global concerns by:

- remembering that you're not always right and finding solutions to conflicts with others
- showing respect for others' feelings; organisations are made up of people who all deserve respect
- knowing when and how to include others and not making other people feel alienated
- being polite to everyone – people of your own age (your peers) and those who are older than you or in more senior positions
- being aware that we are all part of a bigger society. The world doesn't end at your front door, or in your workplace. You need to understand what issues are important to society at large, both nationally and globally, and be aware of pressing issues and willing to contribute. Whether it's awareness of climate change, global poverty or the difficulties that people face in buying a house and getting established in their careers, you should have some idea of what's happening and be willing to form your own opinions about it.

When employers are recruiting new staff, they'll consider a variety of factors. These will include:

- Individual factors: these include your skills and personal qualities, your qualifications and educational experience, work experience, your health and well-being, how willing you are to move to another area, your approach to job seeking, etc.
- Personal circumstances: these include your family responsibilities (for example, it might be harder to find a suitable job if you are caring for young children or a sick relative), the attitude towards work in your family, the degree of support you get from other family members, whether you have a secure home base, etc.

Reproduced with kind permission from the CBI (www.cbi.org.uk).

What Employers Want

Look at what Robert, who runs a busy restaurant, says about his staff.

We employ a lot of young people and my restaurant is where many of them get their first taste of working life. Consequently we're fairly used to the problems that they face when they are starting out like lack of confidence, awkwardness when they're dealing with people, daydreaming, getting flustered, etc. We can train them in the work and most of them shape up fairly quickly and enjoy their jobs. But one of the hardest messages to get across is the importance of being reliable. Some of my staff get it and they turn up come rain or shine, but others have a more casual attitude – if they get a last-minute invitation they'll cancel their shift an hour before it's due to start, which puts a huge burden on everyone else. I understand why it happens – when you're young your priorities are different. But it creates big problems for employers like me. When I'm recruiting staff, I don't care if they are totally inexperienced in restaurant work but I do need to know that they're reliable and will take being employed seriously.

It's important to recognise that you already possess many 'employability' skills. You have gained practical skills and knowledge during your school career that will support you at work. If you've had a part-time job, you'll already understand something about how organisations function and what they expect of employees. For example, if you've been working some evenings and weekends in a restaurant or pub, you'll know how difficult life can be if staff don't turn up for their shifts.

To get started on the career that you want, you need to identify the skills that you already have and present them in such a way that they are recognised. Before you can apply successfully for a job you need to work out what you're already capable of so that you can 'sell' your skills to a potential employer.

In this chapter, we're going to help you evaluate your existing skills and make a list of what you can already do confidently and competently. When you've done this, you'll have a better idea of how to convince potential employers that you're worth considering for a job. You'll also be aware of the areas in which you need to improve your skills.

Who are you and what can you do?

Let's start with a few basics. We're going to ask you to respond to some questions about yourself that will help you establish where you are in your life at this moment in time. Think carefully about each question and make a note of your thoughts on a piece of paper. We suggest that you keep your answers: not only will they give you a starting point for planning future actions and applying for jobs, but you'll also find them fascinating if you look back at them in a few years' time!

You – now!

Your name		Your age	
Where do you live and with whom?			
Describe your education to date: where you went to school/college, and what qualifications you gained.			
Which of your school/college subjects have you found most interesting?			
Which of your school/college subjects have you found least interesting?			

What else do you do at school/college (i.e. extra-curricular activities)?	
What positions of responsibility have you held (e.g. on school council, sports teams, clubs, etc.)?	
What do you do in your spare time (e.g. activities that are not related to school/college)?	
What do you most enjoy doing (be honest – if your favourite pastime is sleeping, admit it!)?	

Your strengths and weaknesses

Next, identify activities that you're good at and the things that you need to improve on. Later in this book we'll show you how to do a SWOT analysis (strengths, weaknesses, opportunities and threats), which is an extension of this exercise.

All about you!

If your friends were describing you, what would they say were your three most likeable personal qualities (e.g. sense of humour, good listener, reliable, etc.)?	

If your teachers were describing you, what would they say were your three best personal qualities (e.g. conscientious student, helps other students, finishes work on time, etc.)?	
If your friends were describing you, what would they say were your three most annoying personal qualities (e.g. talks too much, always late, loud laugh, etc.)?	
If your teachers were describing you, what would they say were your three most annoying personal qualities (e.g. doesn't listen, daydreams in class, etc.)?	

By carrying out these self-assessment exercises, you've started to gather information about yourself. Now we're going to focus on some of the skills that we identified in the previous chapter. At this stage we're only asking you to give a broad assessment of how good you are at these tasks. You'll examine your skills in more detail later.

Look at the statements on the following page and tick the box that most closely reflects your current ability.

What Employers Want

	I'm confident I can do this well	I can do this with help	I'm nervous about doing this	I avoid doing this if I can
Working together and communicating				
Working with other people				
Taking a 'back seat' when required				
Approaching people I don't know and speaking to them				
Listening and accepting other people's opinions				
Letting other people take the lead				
Discussing options and possible solutions to problems				
Speaking on the telephone				
Giving instructions to other people				
Receiving and acting on spoken instructions				
Giving a presentation/speech				
Reading and writing				
Problem-solving and decision-making skills				
Analysing problems				
Collecting and evaluating evidence				
Identifying possible solutions to problems				
Deciding on the most appropriate solution to a problem				
Numbers and ICT				
Simple calculations without using a calculator				
Interpreting data and statistics				
Using a computer for day-to-day tasks				
Using other digital technology (e.g. smart phones)				

Have you surprised yourself with the list of things you can already do? Hopefully this exercise has acted as a confidence booster and helped you to identify just how much you've already achieved.

Providing evidence of your skills and abilities

You've now drawn some general conclusions about your skills and abilities. Any of us can do that; we can all say, 'Oh, I'm good at communicating!' What is important is that you can prove your skill by producing evidence to support that skill.

That is what you'll do next.

Here's an example of someone who is giving clear evidence to back up their claims.

Giving instructions to other people

When I went on work experience in Year 10, I spent a week as a teaching assistant in my old primary school. Most of the time I worked with a teacher in class, but I also volunteered to coach the Year 6 football team. They were very keen but a bit disorganised. I started by gathering them together and giving them a team briefing, describing what we would focus on during a particular session. Then I gave them 10 minutes of warm-up exercises; I divided them into groups, told them what they had to do, then worked with each group individually. When they started playing a game, I coached them from the touchline and at the end of the game we had a short chat about what they'd learned. I had to explain things simply and be very clear about what I wanted them to do. I also had to make sure that they listened to me and understood the instructions. I did this by checking with them and asking individual team members to repeat back what I'd told them.

Looking at the table you completed to analyse your current ability, take one statement from each of the skills lists that you believe you can do well (i.e. a statement where you ticked the first box). Write down a time when you used that skill in a practical situation. You don't need to go into a lot of detail if you don't want to, but try to identify examples to support your claims that you're good at something. Choose four examples from your list and make your notes on a separate piece of paper.

What are your plans?

So far you've focused on what you can do. Now it's time to do some 'blue-sky thinking' and consider what you'd like to do in the future.

Be realistic. For the sake of this exercise, let's assume that you're not going to win the Lottery or a TV talent competition but that you're going to get a job like most people hope to do.

Answer these questions on a separate piece of paper. Put in as much detail as you can.

Your plans

What do you plan to do during the next 12 months?	
Do you plan to continue your education? If so, doing what?	
What sort of job/career are you hoping for when you finish your education?	
What would you like to be doing in 10 years' time?	

To sum it all up ...

Working through the questions in this chapter should have acted as a reality check. It's given you a chance to think carefully about yourself and to focus on what you can do. Most importantly, you've found evidence to support your claims about your skills – and this is key when you start looking for a job.

You've also considered how you'd like the future to work out and the sort of career you're interested in. Now it's important that you bring the two sets of answers together. If you can't find evidence that you are a confident communicator, and you're a bit of a loner, then aspiring to be a teacher or actor is probably unrealistic. If you hate numbers in any shape or form, you won't particularly enjoy a career as a stockbroker – even though you might fancy the rewards.

Keep your answers to this exercise in a file for future reference. As you work through the following chapters, you're going to look at the different skills areas in more detail. Remember that knowledge is power: the more you know about yourself, the easier you'll find it to negotiate the world of work.

First, however, let's examine the other side of the employment equation and consider what employers are looking for when they recruit new staff.

3 Where do you need to be?

Now that you've spent some time analysing what you can already do and where you are now in, let's move on to think about where you need to get to in order to attract potential employers.

One mistake that job-seekers often make is to look at the process of finding employment from their own point of view without considering what the organisations they are applying to require. They forget that an employer is seeking staff because they have a particular vacancy; they need someone to fill a hole in the team or to add extra capability to their existing workforce. Usually organisations don't plan to employ someone because they think he or she will be a fun addition to the workplace/they want to do you a favour/they enjoy the recruitment process!

What do employers need?

Martin is the managing director of a business that rents out holiday cottages. He has more than 50 staff working in administration and in the company's call centre. Here's what he says about recruiting new staff.

We have to think very carefully before we recruit new people even if it's to replace an existing member of staff who is leaving. It's a question of money; staff costs are our main expenditure and we have to monitor them very carefully. So, decisions about how many staff we employ and the jobs they do are taken very carefully and are part of our overall plans for the company.

Our company operates in a rural area where jobs are quite hard to find. I'd love to be able to take on more people because it would help the local community. But there's no point in me taking on staff if, after a few months, I don't have enough work for them or I can't afford to pay them! So, before we recruit or replace staff, we try to work out where the business is going, whether we're expanding or contracting, and whether we'll be able to offer new people job security.

Sometimes it's hard to communicate that to people who are looking for work. They think that because we're a successful organisation that's showing a healthy profit we should be able to offer more jobs. What they forget is that we're profitable because we're careful. We cut our outgoings as much as we can – and that includes keeping the wage bill down.

We need certain staff at certain times. For example, at the moment we have a full quota of administrative staff but we want to take on a new call centre operative. I'd prefer to take on someone who is experienced in this sort of work because training is expensive and takes a long time – new recruits take at least six months to get up to speed and really earn their keep.

Martin's attitude may seem harsh – but he is realistic. If he employed everyone who wanted a job and took on too many untrained staff, he would go out of business within the year. That would put 50 other people out of work.

So remember when you start looking for a job: it's not all about you! It's also about the employer.

What do employers want?

The answer to that question is often quite simple. They're looking for staff they can rely on to do their best, to show willingness and to pull their weight. They don't expect miracles and they don't expect somebody who is straight out of school or college to walk into the workplace and immediately fit in. But employers do want the right sort of attitude.

What does this translate to in real terms? Here's what Martin says.

> When I take on young staff straight from school or college, I'm realistic about what they can do. I don't imagine they'll walk into the office, sit down at a desk and immediately become the company's best sales person. It can take months to learn the ropes, and years to develop good telephone sales skills. I'm prepared for that and the company will provide all the training that is necessary.
>
> What I'm more concerned about is attitude. When I'm recruiting staff I look beyond the qualifications on their CV and their experience. Obviously these things are important – but during an interview I'm also thinking about their personal qualities. Will this person fit in with the other staff? Will they turn up to work every day? Will they take instructions? Will they be reliable?

Remember those personal qualities and attitudes that we looked at in the last chapter? Here some of our interviewees talk about how important they are in real life.

Tenacity and self-control

For many young people who haven't worked full time before, the discipline involved in holding down a job and turning up day after day, week after week, comes as a shock. Yes, you'll get holidays and weekends off – but your working life won't be divided into neat six- or seven-week periods with plenty of recovery time in between, like it was at school.

Yes, we all get sick occasionally. We all get stuck in traffic jams or miss trains and buses. No employer would expect you to turn up when you've got flu or some other genuine illness. What they do expect, however, is that generally you fulfil your work obligations. If you are employed from 9a.m. to 5.30p.m., five days a week, then you should be at work on those days. Simple. So why, for a lot of young employees who are just starting out on their careers, is this a problem?

Neeta has worked in Martin's company for nearly three years. She started as a trainee when she left school after taking her A levels. This is what she said about the difficulties of adapting to working life.

I've always been fairly conscientious and I rarely took time off school. My mum always made sure I was up and ready in plenty of time for the bus, and the school was really strict about attendance so it didn't occur to me to try and disappear for the day.

When I started work it was very different. For a start, the hours were a lot longer and I was really tired. Getting up in the morning was a real struggle and, to make matters worse, my mum decided that it was time I took responsibility for getting myself up and out of the door. If I missed the bus, I was late – and that happened a few times.

The first few months when I started my training were OK. I suppose I was making more of an effort then and everything was new and interesting. But after a while when I'd settled in and the work seemed more routine, I found it harder to get motivated. My attendance record suffered, I had a lot of minor health problems – headaches, colds, that sort of thing – and I admit that I took time off when I really could have gone into work.

After six months I had my first performance review and one of the things that my manager talked to me about was my attendance record. I didn't realise how the days off had added up. More importantly, I hadn't thought about how my absences were affecting the others on my team. They had to cover for me and that often left us short-staffed. In a call centre like the one I work in that's a real problem; if there aren't enough people to man the phones, customers are kept waiting and if that happens too often they go elsewhere.

My manager was very tactful but firm. She told me that I needed to get my act together if I wanted to make a success of this job. I think it was at that point I realised I'd really left school and was now working. My employers were paying me to do a job – and I needed to earn my salary.

Gradually it got easier. I got used to the long days and I did small things to make life more organised, like getting my clothes ready the night before, cutting back on the nights out during the week and turning off my social media sites on the dot at 10p.m. Most importantly, I started to think of myself as part of my work team. I wanted to do my best and earn my colleagues' respect.

I've been with the company for more than two years now and I love my job. I've already been promoted to assistant team leader and I also act as a mentor to new staff that we take on straight from school or college. Many of them have the same problems as I did in getting used to working and being reliable – but my own experiences help me to understand why that happens so I think I'm in a position to help them.

Enthusiasm, flexibility and gratitude

Another quality that employers look for in new recruits is enthusiasm and a willingness to learn. Hairdresser Amanda employs a lot of college students and college leavers in her two salons. Here's what she says about their attitude to work.

Most of the apprentices who come to work here genuinely want to become good hairdressers and they understand that it will take a long time to get the skills that they need. One of the problems

I face, though, is that they find it hard to accept that during their training they'll spend a lot of that time doing fairly menial jobs.

For some of them it's a bit of a shock to start at the bottom, particularly if they've done well at school and college. They're used to being near the top of the tree and suddenly they're back at the bottom, being asked to make the coffee, sweep the floors and sterilise the equipment. Yes, of course they get to do other things and they're continually learning, but a lot of the work in the first few months is fairly basic. The ones who are going to be successful recognise that this is a period that they have to go through and accept it gracefully. But others quickly get bored or resentful and that communicates itself to our customers. I simply can't have someone in my salon who's banging around cups in the kitchen because he or she is fed up at being asked to make yet another cup of coffee. Making that coffee is part of their job and, however boring that might be, I need them to do it with good grace and a smile on their face.

The other problem I've had with trainees and newly qualified staff is that they can be quite rigid in their ideas. I wish I had £10 for every time someone has said to me, 'But that's not how we did it at college/at my last salon.' What they don't appreciate is that every workplace has different ways of working and when you join a company it's up to you to learn those ways and adapt to them, not to impose your own ideas.

One girl who worked for me had a habit of telling me that my techniques were out of date. I honestly think she believed she was helping me by standing in the middle of the salon in front of customers and saying, 'We learned a quicker way to do highlights.' This was not the way to go about it though. It was embarrassing for me and for the clients – and it wasn't doing my reputation any good. I tried to talk to her about it and explain that although I was interested in what she had learned, she needed to talk to me about it in private.

But she didn't get the message – she could get pretty stroppy at times. Needless to say, she didn't last very long. She handed in her notice after six weeks and I've no idea what she's doing now.

It's worth bearing Amanda's words in mind when you start work. Every workplace is different and you must learn how it operates. During your first few weeks watch and listen; don't try to impose your own ideas. And make sure that you observe and learn the routines in the staff room as well as on the 'shop floor'. Mighty battles have started in organisations because of trivial things, like new staff not clearing up after themselves when they've had a coffee or eating all the biscuits!

Watch, listen – and learn.

Humility, respect and good manners

We all act in different ways with different people. Most of the time we do this subconsciously; we know instinctively how to talk to people in an appropriate manner. For example, you wouldn't walk into your head teacher's office and greet them in the same way that you say hello to your closest friend. (At least, we hope that you wouldn't.)

Usually when people start work they are careful about their behaviour and think about what they are saying and doing. However, once you've worked in a place for a while and become used to it, it's easy to forget the rules of polite behaviour. The more comfortable you are, the less formal you are – and that's not always the right way to behave at work.

Here are a few things to remember.

- Think about how you address your colleagues. Don't automatically assume that you can use first names, especially when you're talking to people who are older and more senior than you. In some organisations this is OK and first names are used by everyone from the boss down to the most junior member of staff. In other companies, the more traditional Mr/ Mrs/Ms are used towards more senior or older colleagues. When you start work, listen carefully and see what the preferred terms are. If you're not sure what to call your boss, you can always ask her or him! Most importantly, be polite.

- Don't interrupt people when they're talking. It sounds so simple but it's something that many of us do without being aware of it. We have a question, there's something we need to communicate urgently so we barge in and break up other people's conversations. It's rude, it creates a bad impression and it will annoy the people being interrupted. If you really need to break into a conversation, apologise in advance – and make sure your intervention really is necessary.
- Don't make personal comments about your colleagues or clients. 'My God, did you see that woman's hair/clothes/spots?' might seem like a good talking point with your friends but it's totally inappropriate at work. It is cruel and won't earn you any respect. Keep your opinions to yourself – even if you're asked for them. Try to avoid getting involved in gossip and backbiting at work. It happens all the time but that doesn't mean you have to take part. If you do, you could find that you lose friends rather than make them.
- Be extremely cautious about what you write on any form of social media. A rude comment about your boss or colleagues, or a casual remark that you think your company's latest product is rubbish, can come back to haunt you. Just because your boss is olderthanyoudoesn'tmeans/hecan'tuseInstagramorSnapchat or whatever you're currently using.

So far, we've identified some of the qualities that employers look for in new staff. They also demand particular skills and qualifications and these are the ones that you will see when vacancies are advertised.

Deciphering the job ads

Businesses love jargon! When you have a job and become a member of the 'club' of employed people you'll get used to this and probably start using it yourself. But when you're starting out, it sometimes seems that employers are speaking a foreign language, particularly when they write their recruitment advertisements.

In fact, their requirements are often quite straightforward when you cut through the unfamiliar language. Look at this example of an advertisement for an administrative assistant.

> Whether you're answering queries, filing, working on reception or managing the diary, you'll apply your initiative and positive approach to the crucial, varied work that goes on behind the scenes. Because it's the little things we do which make the overall experience for everyone such a special one. It's a commitment to the kind of visitor experience that will have people coming back again and again. A natural multi-tasker, you'll ideally have worked in a busy office before, so you'll have advanced IT know-how combined with financial skills and a flexible way of working. In short, you'll provide a friendly, professional administrative service across the board.

The key elements of this vacancy are that the successful applicant will:

- want to work in an office (positive approach/provide a friendly, professional administrative service)
- be willing to turn their hand to any tasks as required – and to do more than one thing at a time (natural multi-tasker/ flexible way of working)
- have experience of office work (you'll ideally have worked in a busy office)
- have IT and numeracy/financial skills (IT know-how combined with financial skills).

Don't sell yourself short! Your action plan

Don't be put off by the jargon you encounter in job ads – and don't downplay your own abilities. You may not have all the skills, abilities and experience that employers ask for – but if you can show that you have some of them it's worth making an application for a job.

When a potential employer looks at your CV or application form, or calls you in for an interview, they'll be looking for evidence that you can do what you claim. Anyone can say that they have 'good communication skills' – but you need to prove it. This is where the work that you did in the previous chapter will come in useful. Prepare yourself for your job search by identifying specific examples of things that you've done that show what you're capable of.

So that you remember these, make a list now of the following.

- All the positions of responsibility that you've held.
- All the jobs that you've done, including part-time jobs and work experience. Include brief details of what each job involved.
- Any training that you've received for these jobs. Note how long the training was, when it took place and what topics were covered.
- List any particular skills or knowledge that you've acquired in order to be able to carry out the first two points of this list.

Use the information on this list to help you do the following.

- Complete application forms. If the job asks for a candidate with proven communication skills, identify what you've done that proves you can cope with this demand.
- Write your CV. List your experience chronologically, with the most recent first, and briefly outline what skills you've developed through your work.
- Talk intelligently if you get called for interview. This is your chance to impress a potential employer and they want to know what you can you do – not what you think you can do!

To sum it all up ...

In this chapter, we've considered some of the attributes that employers are looking for in the people they employ.

- Attitude is important – you must really want a job and be prepared to work hard.

What Employers Want

- Employing people is a costly business so organisations can't afford to make mistakes.
- Don't be put off by job advertisements that make long lists of requirements for applicants. If you think you have some of the skills and qualities the employer is asking for, apply.
- You've already done a lot in your life and developed many skills. Spend some time identifying them, and think about how they relate to the job you want to do.
- Be prepared to 'sell yourself' by highlighting the skills that you've developed so far. Always support any claims that you make about what you can do with evidence and concrete examples.

4 Using numbers effectively

What is it about numbers that strikes fear into the hearts of so many people?

Obviously it doesn't affect everyone – you might be one of those fortunate individuals who love numbers, sail through maths exams and don't understand what all the fuss is about. But 30% of people wrongly assume that maths is a skill you are born with, rather than a skill that can be learned.

However, for an awful lot of the UK population, using numbers is something they don't enjoy. To make matters worse, being bad at maths is considered to be acceptable – it's not something we're self-conscious about, as we are if we can't read. Few people would admit happily to being unable to decipher words but many of us will cheerfully say, 'Oh, I've always been hopeless with figures!' when asked to do a simple piece of mental arithmetic.

This has huge implications for our job prospects because numbers underpin so much of what we do.

According to National Numeracy, an independent charity established to help raise low levels of numeracy among both adults and children and to promote the importance of everyday maths skills:

1. Numeracy skills have got worse, not better. The proportion of working age adults in England with skills levels equivalent to GCSE C grade or above was only 22% in 2011.
2. Across the UK roughly four out of five adults have a low level of numeracy.
3. 68% of UK employers are concerned about their employees' ability to 'sense-check' numbers.
4. Lack of numeracy skills is making the country less competitive internationally and costing us billions in lost productivity.

National Numeracy YouGov Survey 2014;
www.nationalnumeracy.org.uk/what-issue

You'll be hard pressed to find a job that doesn't demand some numeracy skills, so it's time to get a grip, throw off your fears and learn to love sums!

What you already know

Ironically many people who complain that they are 'hopeless at maths' have actually been using their numeracy skills efficiently for most of their lives!

We use these skills in everyday situations to do the following.

- Work out how much money we have and what we've spent. As soon as children start receiving pocket money, they start using mental arithmetic to work out the cost of goods and how far their cash will go!
- Plan journeys. If you're travelling by train or bus you'll work out the amount of time the journey takes using the start and arrival time. You'll also use the 24-hour clock, which is another numeracy skill.
- Gauge time and distance. If you decide to visit a friend who lives two miles away and tell him/her that you'll walk over and arrive in 45 minutes, you're actually carrying out a complex sum that involves assessing how much distance you can cover on foot in a particular period of time.
- Work out quantities. When you go shopping for food or household goods, you will mentally calculate how much you need to buy to meet your requirements. So if you're buying the ingredients for a spaghetti Bolognese for four people, you'll work out the amount of meat (about half a kilo), the number of cans of tomatoes you need, how many packets of pasta, etc. And you may well use your conversion skills to switch between metric and imperial weights and measures.

These are just a few examples. The point we're making is that you use your numeracy skills all the time – even though you don't notice you're doing it!

This isn't a maths course and we're not promising to turn you into a mathematical genius. What we want to do is help you to understand why numeracy is so important in almost every workplace.

If you're already confident using numbers and other mathematical principles you may still find this chapter useful because it highlights the ways in which they underpin so many work functions.

It all adds up

At school, as well as learning to use numbers in different ways, you will have learnt other mathematical skills such as algebra and geometry. It's not always easy to see how your school maths lessons relate to everyday life; indeed, you won't use some of the theories you've studied again. At least, you won't use them in their pure, theoretical form – but you may find that they support a lot of tasks that you carry out when you're working and managing your domestic and social life.

For example:

- adding and subtracting when you pay for something in a shop
- calculating dimensions, such as how much fabric or wallpaper you'd need to use when decorating a room
- working out distances between places – and deciding how much petrol you need to put in the car to cover those distances
- weighing, measuring and using the correct temperatures when you're cooking
- using percentages to help you work out how much interest you'll pay on a loan
- scaling amounts up or down using fractions: 'If I'm making half this amount, then I need to halve the ingredients ...'
- converting between Celsius and Fahrenheit temperatures or kilometres and miles
- working out the probability of something happening
- understanding statistical information in the newspapers.

That's only a very small sample. The point is that numbers, like words, underpin almost everything we do. And they are certainly relevant to almost every type of employment.

Numbers at work

When you start work, your employer will train you in the numeracy skills that you need to do your job. So, for example, if you work in an office and take care of some of the accounts, you'll learn how the system works, what calculations you need to do and how to use software packages to make the job easier.

If you work in a business where you handle money and interact with customers – for example, in a shop – your employer will show you the systems that are used. Most retail outlets now use electronic point of sale (EPOS) machines that carry out a range of functions including working out bills, monitoring stock and producing breakdowns of sales. They aren't difficult to use but you'll find it easier to master them if you're confident using numbers. You'll also find it easier to cope if the system breaks down and you have to go back to more traditional ways of working out what customers owe you!

You might be thinking, 'Yes, but I'm planning to be a gardener/work in a stables/teach English. Why do I need to use numbers?' You'll find that numeracy skills are useful in everything you do. Working out how to plan a garden and how long it will take to maintain – you'll use numbers. Estimating and costing food for the horses – you'll use numbers. Marking exam papers and keeping records as a teacher – you'll use numbers.

Jon works in a garden centre. Here he describes some of the ways that his numeracy skills have been put to use.

I don't consciously think about working with numbers – maths wasn't one of my favourite subjects at school and although I got a B at GCSE, I always felt it was something I struggled with. Now that I'm at college, I work here at the garden centre at weekends and during the holidays and I'm using my maths knowledge and skills all the time. What surprises me is how much information I must have absorbed over the years!

When I'm dealing with customers, they often want advice about what to buy and, most importantly, the quantities of products they need. Bags of compost and other products, such as fertilisers, are packed in litres, which doesn't mean much to most people; I need to be able to calculate roughly how much a customer will need to fill the pots in their garden or fertilise the lawn. So, in my head I'm continually converting and working out how far a bag of product will go.

Those conversion skills are used in other ways too. If my boss tells me to prick out some seedlings in three-inch pots and to fill them to a depth of 20 millimetres, I know what she means because I'm used to working with both metric and imperial measures.

Because my job includes working in the shop, I'm handling money all the time. We have an electronic till system but I find it reassuring to also be able to add up amounts in my head. If a customer starts collecting a lot of things to buy, I can keep a running total of how much they've spent and advise them of that before we get to the till. It helps them to monitor their spending – people often get carried away buying plants and garden furniture and don't realise how much everything costs.

Obviously the owner takes care of the books and works out what the business can afford to spend and how much profit we need to make. But all of us are involved to some extent. When I'm working in the shop, I'm aware of what is selling and what isn't, and what mark-up we have on individual products. At the back of my mind, I'm always adding up how much I've sold and whether it's been a good or bad day.

I don't consciously make the links between what I learnt at school and what I do at work. When I'm working out how much turf someone needs to cover their lawn, I'm not telling myself, 'Oh, this is the geometry I learnt in Year 7' or whatever. But it's surprising how much I now use the information that I learnt in the classroom.

In the next section, we're going to focus on some tasks that all of us carry out either at home or at work:

- handling money (counting it, adding up totals, giving change to customers, etc.)
- managing finances
- working with shapes.

Although we're not giving you a crash course in numeracy skills, we can give you some simple techniques that will help you to tackle some of these situations more confidently. And confidence is at the root of many of the problems people face. When you hear someone say, 'I've always been hopeless at maths ever since I was at junior school,' the chances are they're not hopeless – they just think that they are. Think of these techniques as 'tricks of the trade'!

Learn to love numbers

Before you start looking at individual techniques using numbers, let's address a basic principle. **Numbers are easier to use than words!**

Think about it. The English language is full of contradictions. It has rules – then makes exceptions. You have words like 'right', 'write' and 'rite' that sound the same but have totally different spellings and meanings. Language keeps changing. 'Sick' used to mean 'not very healthy' but now ...

The great thing about numbers is that they don't change. They are like blocks of wood that you can move around; you can change the shapes that they make but the blocks remain the same. Number 7 is always number 7.

The same applies to rules that we employ when using numbers. If you learn to multiply, that process of multiplication never changes, even though you might use different numbers. If you learn that $7 \times 7 = 49$ when you're six years old, 7×7 will still $= 49$ when you're 60 years old.

If you can learn to love numbers, you'll find them easier to work with.

Trick of the trade 1

Think of 10 as a magic number. Our whole Western number system is based on multiples of it. We have 10 symbols for numbers, once we reach 100 we start the number sequence over again, percentages use 100 as their base, we measure using a decimal system that is based on units of 10, there are 100 pence in £1 ... 10 is everywhere. Here are some tips.

To multiply a number by 10, add a 0. To multiply a number by 100, add 00.

So, if lemons are 10p each and you want 10 of them, it will cost you £1 (100p).

If you want 100 lemons, they'll cost you £10 (1000p).

Now let's look at using numbers in common situations at work and in your domestic life.

Handling money

If you work in a customer-facing job, then you may be involved in handling cash: counting it, sorting it, converting from one currency to another, giving accurate change, etc.

Sita has worked in retail since leaving school, progressing from shop assistant to assistant manager in a supermarket.

My job is about customer service – and a large part of that is being able to handle money confidently and in such a way that customers feel reassured that their transactions are being handled efficiently. There's nothing worse than going into a shop as a customer and having to correct the salesperson because they got your bill wrong!

My first job was in a small, family-owned general store where most of the sales were in cash so I quickly got used to working out sums in my head. Although the till system works out how much a list of goods costs and tells you the correct amount of change to give back to a customer, the accuracy of the figures is dependent on you putting in the figures correctly so I find that I'm often doing a backup in my head. Obviously, I can't keep a running total of the amount that 20 items will cost – but I will be aware if the total is way out. A lot of the hard work in stores has been removed by computerised till systems – but they can go wrong. On the rare occasions that happens (for example, someone hits the wrong button and messes up a transaction, the electricity goes off, etc.) I can still serve my customers.

As I've moved up the career ladder, I've found that my numeracy skills are in use all the time. One of my jobs is to think about how we can best display goods, where we should put them and how much we need to stock so that we don't run out of popular items or stockpile less popular ones and clutter up the storage areas. Every inch of shelf space is worth money so we have to get our ordering and display right. It's all maths. On a simple level, it's working out how many cans of beans I can fit on a particular shelf. In a large store, that task is multiplied a hundred times. I look at sales information in various retail bulletins and journals to get an idea of what trends are important. So, for example, if sales of product X have increased in the north-west by 20%, this could be a product that we need to stock.

Another task that I'm heavily involved in is forward planning so that I can advise head office what stock we need in the coming months. To prepare for Christmas, I analyse the previous year's sales to find out what sold well and what didn't. I look at the sales figures and number of customers for the relevant period and work out by what percentage they have increased so I can make sure we have sufficient staff at the right times. A lot of this work involves interpreting statistics and being able to make sense of other people's data.

Trick of the trade 2

Here's a tip for quickly adding up those tricky amounts that end in 98p or 99p. If you're adding up a list of numbers that are close to 100, round them up and then subtract the difference.

Here's how it works.

You buy four articles costing £3.99, £2.98, £5.99 and £6.98. You could write all the figures down then add up the columns but it's quicker if you round up each amount to the nearest pound. So, £3.99 becomes £4; £2.98 becomes £3; £5.99 becomes £6; £6.98 becomes £7. Add up those whole pounds; the total is £20.

Now subtract the pennies you used to round up the amounts:

1p + 2p + 1p + 2p = 6p.

Take the 6p away from the £20 and you get £19.94.

The more you use this technique, the faster you'll get. Practise doing this by adding up these amounts.

£12.99 + £15.98 =

£13.75 + £14.99 =

£4.99 + £7.98 =

Managing finance

If you work in a bank or building society, a store that offers finance deals to help customers buy goods, an insurance company, a car dealership or a host of other places where people are involved in fairly large-scale purchases, you may be expected to give advice on offers that are available. To do this, you will draw on numeracy skills that you learnt in secondary school: how simple and compound interest systems work.

Rob works for a car dealership.

Part of my work involves arranging finance for customers who want to buy a car. Not many people can walk in off the street and hand over £12,000 or £15,000 for a new car so we'll help them to find the best deal.

Obviously I've been trained in the various financial products that our business uses but knowledge of the products would be useless if I didn't have a clear understanding of how interest systems work. When a customer is sitting in front of me and we're discussing a finance deal for their new car, I have to make sure they understand exactly what they're signing up for. I have to be able to explain quite complicated figures simply – and I couldn't do that without a reasonably good head for figures.

At school, we learnt about how interest systems on deposits and loans work – and then I promptly forgot about it. I think I was about 14 years old at the time and it didn't seem relevant. But it was all still there somewhere in the back of my brain and as soon as I started my financial training, I knew what the instructors were talking about. It didn't take me long to feel comfortable with the maths in my job – and feeling comfortable makes it easier for me to communicate with my customers.

Understanding how the interest system works is relevant to a lot of your daily transactions, both as a customer and as a supplier of products if you work in an area where finance is involved.

Trick of the trade 3

Percentages are used in a lot of financial transactions because they're a convenient way of communicating increases and decreases.

Percentages are fairly easy to work out once you break them down into blocks using that magic number 10.

To find 10% of a number, divide it by 10. You can do that by moving the decimal point one place to the left. So: 10% of 75 = 7.5.

To get 1%, just repeat the 10% manoeuvre and move the decimal point to the left again: 1% of 75 = 0.75.

You can work out a lot of percentages simply by halving or doubling 1% and 10% of a number and adding up the figures.

You'll find a grasp of percentages useful in any job because it will help you to make quick calculations.

For example, if you're selling a product in the shop you work in for £30 and your boss tells you to put a 5% discount on to it, you can work out the decrease like this:

- 100% = £30
- 10% of £30 = £3
- halve that figure to get 5% = £1.50
- so after the discount is applied, the product will cost £28.50.

If your manager tells you that this year sales are down by 8% compared to last year's total, you can work out what that means in real terms like this:

- last year, total sales were worth £55,000 = 100%
- 1% of those sales = £550
- 8% = 8 × £550 = £4,400
- this year's sales are worth £55,000 − £4,400 = £50,600.

Working with shapes

Remember those shapes and the formulae you learnt to work out angles, circumference, area, etc.? They are some of the most useful principles you'll ever learn because we use calculations based on geometry all the time.

Karim and his sister Neeta have set up a small painting and decorating company. This is what Neeta says.

For the past two weeks, we've been helping with a house renovation project. All the structural work had been done and we were commissioned to do the painting and decorating. One of the most important things we needed to do was to calculate the amount of materials we'd need to decorate each room. If we bought too much of a particular colour paint, that affected our profits. If we bought too little wallpaper and couldn't get extra rolls we were in real trouble. To give the client a realistic estimate up front, we had to work out precise amounts and cost them before we started work. This involved drawing up accurate room plans and calculating the total square footage that we needed to cover. Where we were using wallpaper, we then worked out the number of repeat patterns on a roll and were able to calculate how much wall a single roll would cover. We were also asked to tile the bathroom floor using quite a complicated pattern – I loved that because I got to work out how all the various shapes and sizes of tiles would fit together, putting together rectangles with triangles, etc. You couldn't do this job without a knowledge of geometry. In fact anyone who's proposing to do some decorating needs to understand the basics.

Trick of the trade 4

Here are some simple formulae.

To get the area of a rectangle, multiply the length of the horizontal side by the length of the vertical side. So, if a rug is 6m wide and 4m deep, its area will be 24m².

To get the area of a circle, multiply the length of the radius by itself (to square it), then multiply this figure by 3.14. So, if you want to calculate the area of the top of a table that has a diameter of 60cm, halve the diameter to get the radius of the table (30cm), then square this figure (900cm²). Multiply 900cm² by 3.14. The area of the table is 2,826cm².

To get the area of a triangle, multiply the base by the height and divide by 2. (The height of the triangle is a line perpendicular to the base, from the highest part of the triangle.) So, if a triangle has a base of 12cm, and a height of 8cm, its area will be 96cm².

Using technology with numbers

There was a reason that calculators were invented: they take a lot of the hard work out of using numbers. They also help most of us to calculate more accurately. Obviously, this accuracy is dependent on how well we use the instrument but if you know how to use the calculator's basic functions it will make your life a lot simpler. Adding up, subtracting, multiplying and dividing are straightforward. Equally useful is learning to work out percentages.

Here's an example. Jenny works in a hardware store. Some clients pay cash when they purchase goods, but bigger customers get a monthly account. If the account isn't paid within 30 days, they are charged an extra 8% interest on the amount owed. Jenny has a pile of unpaid invoices to add interest to.

Customer 1 owes £350. This is how she works out the full amount that is now owed using a calculator.

- She puts 350 into the calculator, then presses the 'multiply' key (* or ×).

- She puts 8 into the calculator, then presses the percentage key (%).
- She presses the total key (=). This gives her 28.
- £28 is 8% of £350 and this is the amount of interest that is owed.
- She presses the clear button on the calculator and returns to zero.
- She keys in 350, then +, then 28, then =.
- This gives her a total of £378, the amount that is now owed.

Now work out how much these customers owe when the 8% interest is added to their accounts. Use a calculator.

Customer 2 owes £97.64
Customer 3 owes £175.50
Customer 4 owes £648.00
Customer 5 owes £122.25

Using websites with numbers

f you surf the internet you'll find lots of websites that will help you to carry out simple numerical, algebraic and geometrical calculations. Use them – they're there for a purpose – but be aware that some are more accurate than others. Refer to conversion websites that are part of big sites such as Google or the BBC.

Just remember, though, that when you apply for a job your prospective employer wants to know that you have some numeracy skills and the logic to use them, not that you can simply switch on a machine and get it to do all the work for you. The ability to use mental arithmetic is very important because technology doesn't always work.

Getting help

If you struggle with maths, it's nothing to be ashamed of – but it is an issue you need to address if you want to live both your professional and domestic life to the full. Get extra help as soon as you can. There are lots of sources of help out there including the following.

- Classes. Depending on where you live, you may find numeracy classes in local colleges, careers services and libraries. To find a course go to the National Careers Service course finder website (www.nationalcareersservice.direct. gov.uk/advice/courses). There is also a helpline number on the website so you can talk to someone.
- Online resources. Your first port of call should be www. nationalnumeracy.org.uk – a national charity that helps people of all ages raise their numeracy skills. The BBC has a great website (www.bbc.co.uk/skillswise). This includes sections on using numbers, percentages, fractions, measures, shapes and space and handling data. It is easy to use, and includes activities and worksheets.

To sum it all up (no pun intended) ...

- Numeracy skills are important because they support so many basic tasks that we carry out both at work and at home.
- None of us are born with mathematical skills; we learn them gradually. Consequently, we can continue to learn them when we become adults.
- An employer wants to know that numbers don't frighten you and that you can carry out simple tasks on your own. You will be taught more complex numerical skills that are necessary for your job.
- If you're not confident about your numeracy skills, don't run away from the problem. This is one area that has received masses of government support and you'll be able to find classes locally where you can get help.

5 Using language effectively

Communication skills is one of those 'catch-all' terms that we use frequently but rarely examine. Almost every job advertisement you look at will ask for someone with 'good communication skills' – but few of them specify what these skills actually are.

We're communicating in one way or another from the moment we get up to the moment we fall asleep, so surely we all have these mysterious skills, don't we? Well ... not necessarily. Communicating is about more than talking to your friends and family. It's about:

- understanding the communication cycle that enables us to pass on and receive messages
- speaking in such a way that other people understand what you are really saying
- listening effectively, not just hearing the words that are spoken
- being aware of non-verbal signals that help us understand the true meaning of a message
- being able to communicate in writing in a way that suits the situation that you're in.

In this chapter, we're going to look specifically at that last point. According to the UKCES, one of the functional skills that almost everyone needs to do in almost any job is to use language effectively; they define this as writing clearly and in a way that's appropriate to the context, ordering facts and concepts logically.

In Chapter 9, you'll look at aspects of verbal and non-verbal communication when you're working with colleagues. But for now, let's think about your written communication skills. In these days of instant messaging, texting and other forms of digital communications, you may think that being able to write clearly and fluently is a bit old-fashioned but you'd be wrong. This is a skill that is important to most employers because documentation plays a key role in most jobs.

Can you communicate in writing?

Let's start with a quiz to find out how well you understand the art and science of written communication. Circle the answer that you think is correct, then check your responses. Give yourself five points for every correct answer.

1. You're sending an email with your CV to a prospective employer called Tim Jobsworth. How would you start the email?
   A. Dear Tim
   B. Hi Tim

C. Dear Mr Jobsworth

D. Dear Sir

2. You go to a school council meeting and you're asked to take the minutes. Which activity does this involve?
   A. Taking notes that summarise what happens at the meeting.
   B. Watching the clock and telling everyone the time every 10 minutes.
   C. Writing down every word that is spoken.
   D. Keeping the meeting in order and on schedule.

3. A prospective employer asks: 'Can you use PowerPoint?' Do they want to know if?
   A. You go to the gym and use the wobble board.
   B. You can use a computer program to prepare a presentation.
   C. You can use an electric drill.
   D. You can use a laser-pointing device on a whiteboard in the classroom.

4. Managers often use initialisms (often mistakenly referred to as acronyms) when they communicate. Which of these includes initialisms?
   A. 'Oh, we are happy this morning!' to a miserable-looking colleague.
   B. 'There's going to be a battle with our rival companies before the end of the year.'
   C. 'The CEO of BSB is coming over asap.'
   D. 'He's an idiot, a fool, a dingbat.'

5. You've been offered a better job and you're handing in your notice to your current employer. How would you do this?
   A. In a letter.
   B. By email.
   C. On the phone.
   D. On Facebook.

6. At school you wrote essays; at work you're asked to write a report. What is the key difference between an essay and a report?
   A. A report is shorter.
   B. A report uses bullet points.
   C. A report has a summary.
   D. A report focuses on facts.

7. Grammar and spelling are important – a poorly written document can give a very poor impression. Which of the following is correct?
   A. Gemmas got a new job.
   B. Gemma's got a new job.
   C. Gemma's' got a new job.
   D. Gemmas' got a new job.

8. Emojis are a good way to express your feelings in texts, emails and on social media. When is it appropriate to use emojis in written communications at work?
   A. In an email to colleagues – it will speed up communications.
   B. Never – this is work and emojis are for play!
   C. If you are texting your boss.
   D. All the time – they brighten up the day.

Answers

1. **C** It's a job application, it's formal and you need to be polite. Using his name is better than 'Dear Sir' because it shows that you've read through the application properly and found the name of the relevant staff member to contact. It also stops the email going astray

2. **A** The minute-taker isn't expected to write every word – that would be impossible. But they should make notes about any conclusions, objections, agreements, action points, etc. that are made.

3. **B** PowerPoint software is a standard format for preparing presentation slides.

4. **C** The first is an example of sarcasm, the second is an example of a manager being acrimonious and the fourth shows a number of synonyms. Initialisms are when the initials are used instead of words.

5. **A** Handing in your notice is a formal procedure so you should write a letter so that your resignation is on record. Remember to keep it polite!

6. **D** Reports can be very long and essays can be short so the first answer isn't correct. Although B and C may be true, the main difference between a report and an essay is that a report focuses on facts whereas an essay will include arguments and reasoning.

7. **B** Apostrophes may seem trivial but if they're put in the wrong place, they can change the meaning of a sentence. Misusing them makes you look careless – which will give the wrong impression to whoever is reading your words.

8. **B** Yes, they can be fun but leave emojis (and textspeak) out of the workplace. You never know who will see your emails or texts. When it comes to messaging/emailing/texting/social media, make a strict division between what you do at work and socially.

Check your score

30–40 – Well done! You've already grasped the importance of communicating accurately and appropriately in the workplace. There's always room for improvement so don't skip this chapter.

20–30 – Not bad, but there are areas that you need to focus on. Accept that written communication is important and you need to work at it. Make a note of your wrong answers and learn the correct principles.

Under 20 – Hmm! Maybe you've always thought that accurate written communications are not important – people will always get your meaning. Now you're entering the job market, you need to up your game and recognise that it's your responsibility to get it right. You have work to do!

Why is using language effectively so important?

Unless you're a hermit and never speak to anyone, don't use social media of any kind and refuse to interact with the rest of the human race, you'll know the answer to this question already. We use language and communication skills to let other people know who we are and what we want; we also use these skills to find out about other people and what they want.

When you're young, you get a lot of leeway in the way you use language – adults make an effort to understand you. Think about what happens at school.

- If you're talking to your friends, the chances are that you all speak the same language, use the same slang. You mix with a relatively small circle of people who are the same age as you, so they're aware of the codes that you use in your speech, writing and body language. They understand LOL on a text, that you're not being deliberately rude when you don't raise your eyes from your mobile during a conversation, that yawning isn't necessarily a sign that you're bored.
- If you're in class and you're trying to answer a question, your teachers may often help you out by supplying you with words or clarifying your statements.
- If you submit a piece of written work, the teacher will look as much at the content as at your presentation and spelling.

When you start work, however, the standards are different and the way in which you communicate becomes much more important.

In the workplace, we communicate with our bosses, the people who work for us, our clients, potential customers, suppliers, authority figures ... the list goes on and on. Many of these people are older and from different backgrounds; they don't share your 'language' and it's up to you to learn theirs.

Many of the problems that arise in the workplace are the result of poor communications. Here are some examples.

- A supervisor doesn't give instructions clearly and the person doing the job gets it wrong.
- A new member of staff doesn't listen to instructions and crashes the IT system.
- A shop assistant is having a bad day and speaks abruptly to a customer, who takes offence and tells all her friends to boycott the store.
- A letter to a prospective client is badly written and misspelt so the client looks for another supplier who is more careful.
- Senior managers don't tell their staff about changes that are planned for the organisation so the workers rely on rumours for information and threaten to go on strike.

These are just a few examples to illustrate why communication of all kinds and at all levels is so important.

In February 2016, the Department for Business Innovation and Skills (DBIS) published a research paper, 'Impact of Poor Basic Literacy and Numeracy on Employers'. The paper states:

> One in eight (12%) workplaces in England report a literacy and/or numeracy
> gap whereby at least one member of staff is unable to perform certain
> literacy or numeracy tasks to the level required in their day-to-day job …
>
> www.gov.uk/government/uploads/system/
> uploads/attachment_data/file/497544/BIS-16-36-impact-
> of-poor-basic-literacy-and-numeracy-on-employers.pdf

The DBIS suggests that this percentage may be on the low side because many employers don't recognise the full scale of the problem within their organisations.

The cost of this basic skills gap is very high for employers; it affects productivity, can compromise health and safety and demotivate the workforce. The cost is equally high for the employees who have difficulties with basic skills; it can make them feel inferior and limit their progress at work. The DBIS paper staes that:

> … between a third to a half of employers with a basic skills gap reported an increase in the number of errors made by staff, a constraint on the introduction of new and/or more efficient processes, and/or a reduction in product or output quality.

The problems related to using language effectively are not just about people who have difficulty with basic skills and find reading and writing challenging. One of the constant gripes in the professional world is that well-educated staff, many of them graduates, cannot communicate in writing without making glaring errors. These affect the credibility of the organisation. How would you feel if your son or daughter brought home a letter from the teacher and it was full of spelling mistakes?

In this section, we're going to consider a range of reading and writing training that you received at school and consider why it is important in the workplace. Were all those rules of grammar and spelling just a form of antiquated torture that teachers devised to make your life a misery, or do they have a purpose? And if you are experiencing problems, what can you do about them?

The importance of clarity

Written communication is harder than face-to-face communication because the person you are addressing only has the words on the paper to refer to. There is no body language, no tone of voice, no questions and answers to help clarify matters, just a set of symbols. When you're talking to someone you can continually check back that they understand your meaning; when you write to them you have no idea how they will receive your words. For this reason, it's essential that written communication is accurate and clear, and that it doesn't leave room for misinterpretation.

The following examples, taken from Jan Veniola's book *Write Right* (1991), show what happens when you get it wrong. There are also a few from a typical work environment that have been added in. Can you spot what is wrong with these sentences and how they should have been written?

He told her he wanted to marry her frequently.

We saw a man on a horse with a wooden leg.

The sunbather watched the soaring seagull wearing a striped bikini.

The fire was extinguished before any damage was done by the Fire Brigade.

At the age of five, his father died.

Walking along the shore, a fish suddenly jumped out of the water.

The assistant took the paper out of the printer that was ripped.

He pulled at the cable for his computer under his desk.

The pay rise came from her boss for her good work.

He told her he wanted to marry her frequently. So what was this man doing: telling his girlfriend every day that he wanted to marry her, or wanting to get married to her every Saturday? The meaning would be clear if this was rewritten as: *He told her frequently that he wanted to marry her.*

We saw a man on a horse with a wooden leg. How many horses with wooden legs have you seen? This should be rewritten as: *We saw a man with a wooden leg on a horse.*

The sunbather watched the soaring seagull wearing a striped bikini. A seagull wearing a striped bikini is an interesting idea but this should be rewritten as: *The sunbather wearing a striped bikini watched the soaring seagull.*

The fire was extinguished before any damage was done by the Fire Brigade. This suggests that the Fire Brigade were likely to cause damage. It should be rewritten as: *The fire was extinguished by the Fire Brigade before any damage was done.*

At the age of five, his father died. If his father was only five when he died, how could he be a father? This should be rewritten as: *When the boy was five, his father died.*

Walking along the shore, a fish suddenly jumped out of the water. This suggests that the fish was walking along the shore and simultaneously jumping out of the water. It should be: *When I was walking along the shore, a fish suddenly jumped out of the water.*

The assistant took the piece of paper out of the printer that was ripped. In this sentence it seems as though it is the printer that is ripped. It should be: *The assistant took the ripped piece of paper out of the printer.*

He pulled at the cable for his computer under his desk. We need to make it clear that it's the cable and not the computer that is under his desk. It should be: *He pulled at the computer cable that was under his desk.*

The pay rise came from her boss for her good work. Is it the employer's good work or the boss's that has brought about the pay rise? To make it clearer it should be written like this: *The pay rise for her good work came from her boss.*

These few examples illustrate the problems that arise when sentences are not written correctly: the meaning is unclear and the resulting mistakes create howlers that will damage the credibility of the writer. They can also cause serious problems at work. Many people are offended by poorly written English because they equate it with a careless attitude and a lack of respect for the reader. If these people are your customers or your bosses, then you will not be able to build a positive relationship with them.

Although we may learn some grammar at school, most of us are not examined on our knowledge of dangling modifiers! But in our English lessons at school we are encouraged to write correctly so that using the right structures becomes automatic and we can instinctively spot an error. Mistakes like the ones above can be avoided by reading back what you have written before you print it or send it to someone else.

Next we're going to look at specific areas of written communication that are used frequently in the workplace and relate them to work that you've already done in school or college.

Letters

One of the key problems that we face with written English is that the language is constantly changing. You do not use the same vocabulary and sentence structure as your parents and grandparents; times move on and so do the ways in which we communicate. However, this can cause major difficulties if one section of the population is communicating in a way that another section cannot, or does not want to, understand.

This is what Greg, the director of an insurance company, says about the importance of written communication in his company.

Our business is based on accurate communication: clients have to understand what their policies offer so we have to be able to tell them in terms that they can follow easily. Obviously we talk to them in person or over the phone about their insurance cover, but then we have to put down the terms and conditions in writing so that the customers have the chance to sit down and study them and make sure they are getting what they need.

If my staff don't have a sufficient grasp of written English, they won't understand the documentation so they have no way of knowing if the cover is correct. It's important that they can read a fairly complicated document, which may be written in formal language. They also need to be able to work with unfamiliar vocabulary and make sense of it.

It's also important that they can put together letters and other documentation in such a way that customers feel confident that they are receiving a professional service. Many of our customers have high standards; they come from a generation where the rules of grammar and spelling were important. If we send out a letter that is not written correctly, it suggests a certain shoddiness that they may suspect reflects our business as a whole – and that's not good.

I remember one account handler arguing with me that traditional forms of address in letters, like following Dear Sir with Yours faithfully, were out of date and no longer important. Well, in a formal situation I believe that they are. Whether you like it or not, whether you think it's old-fashioned and no longer relevant, the fact remains that there are rules to language that many people still observe. And they get very upset if we don't observe them too.

Greg's point is important. As he says, when you're writing for professional purposes it is what matters to your customer that is important, not what matters to you. So although your normal form of address in a note or an email might be *Hi mate* or *Hello Mr Smith*, you may inadvertently cause offence. Mr Smith may place a great deal of importance on the way that written communications are structured because he believes that they reflect the efficiency and thoroughness of the company.

At school you were probably taught the basic rules of letter writing:

- how to address people whose names you know (Dear Mr/Mrs/Ms X with a closing line of Yours sincerely)
- how to address people whose names you don't know (Dear Sir/Madam with a closing line of Yours faithfully)
- where to place the addresses of the sender and the recipient, and the date, on a formal letter.

Although these rules may be largely irrelevant to your everyday communication because you rarely write a letter and communicate entirely by email or text, they are still important in business. This includes writing letters formally and following the rules when you are preparing covering letters for job applications. Many employers won't consider reading a CV or application form if the covering letter is badly presented and structured because they suspect that this carelessness reflects on the applicant's character. Harsh – but true!

Comprehension

Remember those comprehension exercises that you did as part of your GCSE English Language course? The ones where you were given something to read then asked to answer questions on it?

If you think back, you've actually been practising your comprehension skills since you started primary school – and for a very good reason. Comprehension means understanding and comprehension exercises are designed to test your understanding of something that you read. This is something that you will need to do in almost every aspect of your life. Whether you're reading a newspaper article, a legal document, a set of instructions, an advertisement or a report, you need to be able to process the words and extract the meaning behind them.

One popular approach to improving your reading and comprehension skills is the SQ3R approach. SQ3R stands for five steps that you can use when reading something that you want to remember.

- **Survey.** This gives you an overview of the text. Look at the title, contents page, summary. Think about the main points in the text and how it is laid out. This will give you a clue about how the author has arranged ideas and what is important.
- **Question.** Ask yourself what information in the text will be useful to you. At this stage you should be able to tell which parts you need to read carefully and which you can skim through.
- **Read.** Once you have decided to read a section, read it slowly with your full concentration. Paragraphs contain 'chunks' of meaning, so make sure you understand the meaning in

those chunks. Highlight words and phrases that you do not understand.

- **Recall.** To make sure you've understood what you have read, recall the main points by making a note of them. This will help you develop your understanding.
- **Review.** Now you should be able to bring together what you have read and what you want to know/are studying. You should be able to follow the argument and you should understand the content of the text. If you can't do this, go back to the text and use a dictionary to look up unfamiliar words and phrases and reread if necessary.

Remember, reading is a skill like writing that you will develop if you are purposeful and systematic.

In many cases, you may also have to communicate that meaning to other people in a way that they understand.

Look at what Melissa says.

I'm a manager in a pub. That's not the sort of job you'd immediately associate with a need for good reading and writing skills but the amount of paperwork I get through every week is enormous. We get reports from the brewery, letters from our suppliers, piles of paper about the legal side of the business – licensing, health and safety, etc. – and it has to be read and understood. I also have to make sure that the staff are kept up to date. If something goes wrong, ignorance isn't an excuse. An important part of my job is to read through all the stuff that comes in and to sort out what is relevant to my bar staff. Because we have a lot of part-timers working in the pub, it is hard to get everyone together for staff briefings. I prepare a newsletter every week that highlights the most important points they need to be aware of and make sure that every member of staff gets a copy and reads it.

> Like a lot of people, at school I couldn't see the point of all those endless comprehensions – but now I'm putting the skills that they taught me to good use. I can read a document and summarise the key points and I'm not fazed by complicated or lengthy papers.

Reports

As well as comprehension exercises, you'll also have practised your writing skills in your English lessons. Many of the things that you wrote, whether it was an account of a place that you visited, an event in your life, or something you saw or heard, are actually reports. They are reporting your experiences or other types of information to another person.

Reports are a common feature of almost every workplace for exactly the same reason: they are a means of communicating information to others. And the rules that you learnt about effective report writing at school are just as important when you write professional reports.

See what Greg, the insurance company director that you met earlier in this section, says.

> Reports are a key part of our business. There is no way you can gather everyone you want to speak to in one place at one time, so we rely on written reports to communicate with them. We prepare reports for our customers about the products that are available to them. We prepare reports for the directors of the company to tell them about the way the business is performing. We prepare reports for staff so that they are aware of information that is important for their job. We prepare reports for the media, like local newspapers, to tell them about company developments.

Effective reports – and most other types of writing, for that matter – usually have three clear sections:

1. an *introduction* that tells the reader what it is about
2. the *development*, in which the subject is explored in detail
3. a *conclusion* that sums up what has been said and may suggest further action.

In simple terms, an effective piece of writing will usually: 'Tell them what you're going to tell them, tell them, and tell them what you've told them!'

If you think back, this is probably a structure that you were taught many years ago when you first started to write extended pieces of prose. It's not a complicated process- but it's surprising how many people struggle to get it right.

An important feature of a good report is its length: keep it as short as you can. There are two reasons for this.

1. Reports are usually read by busy people who don't have time to wade through pages of irrelevant material.
2. The more you write, the more likely you are to go 'off message', to deviate from your key points and confuse your audience.

Before you write a report

There are a number of ways to organise a report before you start to write the actual words and, again, many of these will be familiar from your schooldays.

- List headings and bullet points and group these together.
- Don't try to cover too much in one report and stick to the essential information.
- Try making mind maps or spidergrams to get you started, then group the key facts/ideas together.
- Write a summary that you can use as the basis for your report. The summary can consist of a series of single sentences.

When you're writing the content

- Distinguish between facts and opinions so that readers know what is true and what is speculation.
- Keep it short and simple (KISS). Keep your sentences and paragraphs short, and never use a complicated word or sentence structure when a simple one will do.
- Use headings, subheadings and bullet points to break up long paragraphs of text – it makes the report easier to read.
- Avoid jargon and initialisms, even if you think your readers will probably understand them. Clear meaning is all important and it's hard to achieve that if you're using terms and phrases that could confuse your reader. Also, using jargon can be interpreted by some readers as a form of aggression. By using words and phrases that they may not understand, you're suggesting that they are not part of the elite or in-crowd that share this exclusive language.

After you've written your report

- Read it again. Is the meaning clear? Will all your readers understand it?
- Proofread your work, just like you were taught to check through a piece of writing before you submitted it to a teacher. Spelling mistakes and bad grammar not only irritate readers who spot them, they also suggest that you are careless and that is not a good image to cultivate.
- Try to put yourself in your readers' shoes. Is your message clear? Is it clear what has happened and what should happen next?
- Ask yourself: have I used the best form of presentation to convey my message? A picture, diagram or chart can make more sense than words and all of these formats are available in most word-processing packages.

Above all, when you are writing letters or reports remember that, as with all other forms of communication, what matters is serving the needs of your audience – not yourself.

Emails, blogs, texts and other forms of digital communication

We are living through a period of time when communications have been revolutionised by new technology. You probably communicate with most of your contacts by text, email or some other form of instant messaging. You may have your own website, be a regular blogger and spend a lot of time on Facebook and Twitter. If so, you'll be aware of the key advantage of these communication media – speed.

A lot of companies have recognised that they need to adapt their own written communication systems to take advantage of the technology that is available. At the time of writing, Twitter has more than 300 million monthly active users, Instagram has 500 million and Facebook has 1.59 BILLION monthly active users. It's not surprising that companies use these facilities as part of their business communications when they can reach such large audiences in a matter of minutes. Companies use the service as a marketing and public-relations tool and include links that take people back to corporate web pages, press releases and other promotional sites. Starbucks is a good example of an organisation that does this. They develop close relationships with customers through social media, post information about special offers and even have a dedicated section of their website where customers can post ideas about how to improve the company's service and products.

However, if you're using these communication methods as part of your work you need to recognise both the pros and the cons. Emailing or texting customers is not the same as emailing or texting your friends.

One of the biggest drawbacks with instant communications is that the speed that makes them such an asset can also lead to careless mistakes. A badly written email in answer to a complaint can alienate a customer. An email that is sent out then not followed up can create bad feeling and a lack of trust.

An email or text that is sent out for work purposes needs to be as carefully considered as a letter. It must be polite, address the important issues and be clear in its meaning. You might communicate fluently in text speak but your recipient may not, so using common abbreviations is risky.

"2 b, r nt 2 b dat iz d Q wthr ts noblr n d mnd 2 sufr d slngs & arowz of outrAjs fortn r 2 tAk armz agnst a C f trblz, & by oposn nd em?" might make perfect sense to you, but it doesn't to everyone. (If this has you confused, here's the translation: "To be, or not to be: that is the question: / Whether 'tis nobler in the mind to suffer / The slings and arrows of outrageous fortune, / Or to take arms against a sea of troubles / And by opposing end them?")

Emails and texts also need to be sent to the right person. There have been countless examples of the wrong emails being inadvertently sent out to the wrong people – or, worse still, confidential emails being sent to too many recipients.

Bear in mind that the protocol for emails and texts at work is different to that in personal situations. These forms of communication take time to prepare and read. That might not be important when you're sitting at home watching TV with one eye and carrying on a text conversation with your best friend with the other. At work, however, time is money, and non-essential communication can distract people from what they should be doing. Keep messages brief and to the point, and don't send them unless they are essential.

Finally, be cautious in what you put on social media. Yes, of course you have the right to post pictures of yourself on holiday or at a party when maybe you weren't on your best behaviour. Just remember that anything you post for the world to see may be seen by your boss. There are countless examples on the internet of people who lost their jobs because of social-media posts. Some of them are hilarious – but not for the now unemployed men and women who were too quick to share.

To sum it all up ...

- Written communication is an essential part of business and most employers will expect you to be able to read documentation associated with your work and to write clearly and accurately.

- If you feel that you need help, particularly with your written-communication skills, you will find free classes available via learndirect, a UK organisation that promotes learning and development. Check out its website (www.learndirect.co.uk). Alternatively you can find information about online and face-to-face classes through www.nationalcareersservice.direct.gov.uk/advice/courses.

- Social media is one of the great developments of our age but use it with caution. It's very easy to give the wrong impression of yourself – and you never know who's watching.

- Finally, stop making excuses. Don't try and hide behind statements like, 'Oh, I was always hopeless at English', or 'I'm better at talking than writing'. When you're working, excuses don't do you any favours. It's time to make an effort and improve this vital skill.

6 Using ICT effectively

Many of you who are reading this book will have been using computers for years. They will be an integral part of your life in school or college and at home. You probably have your own laptop or tablet, and you use your smartphone to access the internet as well as make calls.

However, for some of you, information and communication technology (ICT) may hold little charm. You may find computers intimidating because you can't understand how they work. You may simply have little interest in interacting with a machine. Or you may have never had time to hone your ICT skills because you were too busy doing other things.

What Employers Want

Unfortunately, if you belong to the latter group, this could cause you problems when you're at work because ICT is a feature in most workplaces.

In 2016 the BCS (was the British Computer Society, now the Chartered Institute for IT) stated:

What do employers want from their employees?

According to our recent survey of HR professionals and employers, 90% rate operating a digital device as important to the majority of roles in their organisation. Today almost every job relies on some aspect of technology: whether it's sitting at a PC in an office, working at a checkout or delivering parcels.

Employers want people to have the skills to be productive straight away in a new role and believe digital skills improve employee efficiency and increase business productivity.

Why is digital literacy important to employers and employees?

Key findings in our survey showed that:

- 81% of employers regard digital skills to be an important requirement when employing people
- 97% felt email skills are important to the majority of roles in their organisation, along with:
  - Word processing (92%)
  - Spreadsheets (89%)
  - Social media (71%)
- 68% rated increased efficiency as one of the top two benefits of digital literacy for employees.

www.bcs.org/category/17854

In this chapter, we're going to look at what employers mean when they ask for 'ICT skills' or demand that candidates for jobs are 'IT literate'.

We're going to look at the most commonly used software applications and explain what they do and why you could be asked to use them in a job. Rather than ask you questions and present you with quizzes to assess your competence, we are giving you a series of checklists so you can identify what skills you already have. This will help you to assess whether or not you are ICT proficient in all areas, and decide whether you need further training.

Why is ICT important in the workplace?

'ICT' (or 'IT') refers to any technology or process that will store, retrieve, manipulate, transmit or receive information electronically. It covers personal computers, digital television, email, data-storage equipment, robots, mobile phones, etc.

The great thing about ICT is its capacity to deal with massive amounts of information quickly and efficiently. It takes the strain out of processes, it improves productivity, and it is very, very fast.

Think about how you've used ICT in school or college to help you complete assignments. If you have access to a computer you can:

- carry out research online and access far more data than you could in a library
- consult with other people via websites and email to get more information
- draft out ideas and alter them without having to rewrite the whole document from scratch
- prepare a final version and format it so that it looks attractive
- carry out spelling and grammar checks
- circulate your work to a number of people for review and comment
- store your work so that it can be retrieved at any time.

Now let's repeat the assignment process without access to ICT.

- You'll have to go to the library (if you still have one locally) to find books for your research – if they are available and not already out on loan.
- If you want to talk to someone about your ideas, you'll have to phone them and take notes about what they say as you speak.
- You'll make notes by hand. These will have to be stored and at some point translated into the content of your assignment.
- You'll have to write a final version by hand. If it gets untidy, you'll end up writing it out again.
- Spelling and grammar checks will be dependent on your command of written English! If you're lousy at spelling you're not likely to spot all the errors.
- If you want to circulate your work, you'll have to get it photocopied then post it off and wait for it to be returned. Then you'll have to collate all the comments and write another final version incorporating those comments.
- Finally you'll have to find somewhere to keep your old assignments – or throw away all that hard work.

ICT improves your speed, the breadth of your knowledge and your final product. Obviously nothing is perfect and there are drawbacks; some people argue that ICT makes students lazy, over-reliant on other people's opinions and unable to think for themselves. But whatever your viewpoint, you can see that there are advantages.

Exactly the same situation exists in the workplace. ICT can improve performance *provided* that it is used properly.

We talked to three people about the ways in which ICT enhanced their work. We deliberately chose individuals whose jobs are not dependent on ICT but who choose to use it.

Gregg is a farmer in his late 40s.

> I came late to using computers and I admit I fought against them for a long time – it was my kids who got me started. But in the last ten years it's transformed the way we work. Our farm is quite isolated but online I have instant access to any help that I need – from official bodies such as the Health and Safety Executive and the Department of Environment, Food and Rural Affairs through to website forums where I can get advice from other farmers. We do all of our ordering online, we monitor productivity and milk yields, we've got databases of clients, we do the accounts – all the day-to-day running of the farm.

Kate is a florist.

> I suppose I could develop my own spreadsheets, order forms and everything else I need, but I work long enough hours as it is! I'm up at 3a.m. if I'm going to the flower market and I can be preparing orders all night before a wedding so I wanted a way to streamline some of the routine tasks. I found a software package that gave me an efficient order taking and processing system, set up a database of clients, prepared order forms and invoices. It included an accounts package, which has really helped because I can program it in different ways, get statements and reconcile my accounts. I reckon that using the package saves me at least eight to ten hours' admin a week and gives me more time to do the job that I love – arranging flowers.

Working in a related field, Jon is a garden designer.

> I used to draw up plans for clients' gardens by hand which was fun but time-consuming and there was always scope for them to say the finished garden wasn't what they'd expected. Now I use a computer-aided design package and it's transformed the way that I work. I can create detailed plans that have a 'walk-through'

facility so clients see exactly what they're going to get. These can be linked to planting plans and costings. It's taken a lot of the guesswork out of what I do, as well as speeding up the process.

Like our interviewees, many small- and medium-sized companies buy packages 'off the peg' that can be used with PCs or Apple Macs. They use software that you may already be familiar with because it's similar to the software you use at home or at school.

Bigger systems

Larger organisations will probably have their own IT departments that develop 'bespoke' software that is specially equipped to deal with the company's business. Consequently, it may be unfamiliar and you'll have to learn new skills and techniques to use it.

Bear in mind that the IT used in industry and commerce will be expected to do a lot more than your average word-processing and spreadsheet package. IT is used to link people and business functions across the globe and it can be extremely complex.

Fortunately, you will rarely be expected to understand the intricacies of the system unless you're actually planning a career in IT development or maintenance. What you do need to be able to do is master the IT that applies to your particular job. So, for example, if you work in retail you should understand the principles of the electronic point of sale (EPOS) system and be able to use the hardware efficiently. If you work in an office and process simple accounts, you should be able to use a spreadsheet. If you work in a design company, you could be expected to use Photoshop or Quark. And everyone should be able to use email and access the internet.

Word processing

Computer companies exist to make a profit not to make life easy for you. This means that there are a number of different word-processing packages on the market. The most commonly used one on PCs is Microsoft Word. But just to make sure that those profits keep on rolling in, Microsoft regularly updates its programs and adds in new fiddly bits. As soon as you feel comfortable with a word-processing program you may find that your employers update the system and you have to start learning all over again. That's life.

Employers use word-processing packages to:

- create, save and retrieve documents such as letters
- format documents using templates (for examples, letters, reports, etc.).

Checklist

Use this checklist to identify any shortfalls (areas that you need to revise or improve on). Tick the boxes for the tasks that you already feel confident performing.

I can:

Open a word-processing program	
Navigate the tool bars on the system that I'm using	
Retrieve and open documents	
Save documents	
Store documents in relevant folders	
Create a document using a template	
Use the Help menu	
Recover a document if the system stops responding	
Adjust page settings (margins, tabs, etc.)	
Copy and move text	
Find and replace text	
Create and use tables	
Use reviewing tools such as track changes	
Add headers and footers	
Insert page numbers, date and time	
Use the spell-check facility	
Insert symbols	
Preview a document before printing	
Print a document	

Simple design techniques

If you get a job that involves designing documents, you should receive training in the skills that you'll need. However, most word-processing packages offer the facility so that all of us can get creative and make our documents look more interesting. This can range from allowing us to drop a photograph into a letter, through to designing a leaflet.

Checklist

Use this checklist to identify any shortfalls (areas that you need to revise or improve on). Tick the boxes for the tasks that you already feel confident performing.

I can:

Locate and insert pictures from galleries such as Clip Art	
Locate and insert photographs from my own files	
Add styles to a picture/photograph	
Apply picture effects	
Modify picture size	
Create stylised text using a program such as WordArt	
Insert and create charts	
Add shapes to documents	

Spreadsheets

Spreadsheets (also called worksheets) display numerical information in rows and columns. They can be used in any area that works with numbers and are commonly found in the accounting, financial-analysis and scientific fields.

Spreadsheets are used a lot in business because they make formatting and retrieving information so easy. With a program such as Microsoft Excel, you can organise, analyse and present data quickly and efficiently. Employers use this software to manage payments and orders, to work out their accounts and VAT and for a hundred other functions.

Worksheet/spreadsheet packages are often modified by users so that they perform particular functions. It's unlikely that your employer will expect you to be a spreadsheet wizard the day you start work. If your job involves using these applications you should be trained and given plenty of time to practise using them.

Checklist
Use this checklist to identify any shortfalls (areas that you need to revise or improve on). Tick the boxes for the tasks that you already feel confident performing.

I can:

Open and save a worksheet	
Move around a worksheet	
Enter labels and values on a worksheet	
Edit labels and values on a worksheet	
Select rows, columns and special ranges	
Manipulate worksheets (copy, move, hide, etc.)	
Use simple formulas to perform calculations (add, find averages, etc.)	

Presentation software
You should be familiar with presentations from school or college. The days when teachers scrawled on the blackboard using chalk are long gone and most teachers now use interactive whiteboards and/or presentation software in class.

You may also have used this software to prepare presentations at school/college, perhaps as part of a project. If you've worked with the most commonly used packages, such as PowerPoint, you'll know that they are easy to use. Effectively, you just type up the points you want to make and the software converts your words into slides.

Presentations offer many advantages. People retain more information when they get a chance to look and listen, so talking and showing slides or pictures will help to get your message across. You can insert interesting pictures, visuals, spreadsheets, etc. to make your message clearer. Most packages will also allow you to print off handouts so that information can be circulated and retained after the presentation is finished.

It's important to recognise, however, that presentation software is an adjunct to your presentation; it doesn't replace you, the presenter. Your slides should show only the key messages that you want to convey, not every word that you intend to speak.

The key to making a good presentation is to keep your visuals simple. Try to include too much information on a slide and it will become illegible. Add too many visuals, graphics, fonts, colours and special effects and you'll detract from the message. You should include only relevant information, leave lots of white space and focus on making it easy to read.

Again, your employer is unlikely to ask you to prepare a presentation for the board of directors on your first day at work unless you've been specifically employed to do this sort of thing and have previous experience. However, you might be asked to contribute to presentations fairly early on in your career because they are such a popular method of communication.

Martin, the managing director of the holiday cottage rental business, whom you met in Chapter 3, describes the role that presentations – and presentation software – play in his company.

Like many companies, we include presentations during staff briefings so that everyone is up to speed on what is happening in the business. These can be given by anyone in the company who has something relevant to say, so one week it might be the sales director talking about targets for the coming year and another week it could be a trainee giving a presentation to encourage staff to take part in activities to raise money for charity.

Additionally, we organise a lot of open evenings for prospective clients – the people who might want to rent out a cottage. We want to show them the types of property that we deal with and the benefits they'll get if they use us as agents. We use presentation software to make these occasions interesting and informative; we can convey a lot more information about the business through showing pictures of properties and satisfied customers than we can through words.

A lot of these presentations are given by either me or section managers, but we rely on other staff to help us prepare them. That includes some of the junior account handlers and call-centre staff. I like to know that all the people who work here have as wide a skills base as possible and that they're not intimidated by technology. We train them on various systems when they start working with us – and that includes a course on using PowerPoint. I'm aware that the young woman or man who has just started manning the phones this month could be a team leader in a couple of years' time. When that happens they'll be presenting regularly to their staff and need to be fully confident, so the earlier they start using the presentation software, the better.

Checklist

Use this checklist to identify any shortfalls (areas that you need to revise or improve on). Tick the boxes for the tasks that you already feel confident performing.

I can:

Browse through a presentation and switch between slides	
Create new slides	
Insert text and graphics onto slides	
Insert and modify tables	
Add animation (e.g. introduce objects onto the slide one at a time)	
Rehearse timings to control the amount of time each slide appears on screen	
Prepare handouts	

There are many other functions that even the most simple presentation software can now be used for. For example, you can add voice-overs or set the presentation to run automatically.

Database programs

You will already be familiar with using simple databases: for example, your contacts list in your mobile phone is a database. In a work context, organisations rely heavily on databases to store information about their clients, suppliers, and every other aspect of their business. They are the modern equivalent of huge filing cabinets in which data can be stored and easily accessed.

Database programs allow you to store, manage and organise information in a way that makes it easily accessible. This information can be retrieved in a variety of formats that combine data, text and graphics. It can also be updated quickly and easily.

Basically, databases use tables, just like spreadsheets. Just like spreadsheet tables, database tables have columns and rows. Each column contains a different type of attribute (e.g. first name, age, first line of address); each row makes up a single record (all the information about a particular person or object).

So why can't you just store information on spreadsheets? The advantage with a database is that it allows you to manipulate the data and retrieve it as you need it. You can also carry out a range of tasks, such as updating and cross-referencing.

Think about a simple database that contains the names, addresses, telephone numbers, email addresses and birthdays of all your contacts. Using one simple command you can instruct your computer to show you all the information that you need at any one time; for example, using one command you could identify all of the people who have birthdays in a particular month; using another command you could list the telephone numbers; using another command you could print out address labels, etc. That saves you having to trawl through page after page of tables to find out what you need to know. You can also get more general information from the database (e.g. how many people are listed) in a report.

Entering information into a database, manipulating it and retrieving it is easy once you know how and you may already be familiar with some of the most popular database programs, for example Microsoft Access. Individual companies often have their own systems, however, and you will need to be trained in using these.

If you claim that you are experienced in using database programs you should be able to carry out basic tasks, such as the ones in the checklist below.

Checklist

Use this checklist to identify any shortfalls (areas that you need to revise or improve on). Tick the boxes for the tasks that you already feel confident performing.

I can:

Create and save a blank database	
Create a table by entering data	
Work with database objects	
Add new data to a database	
Delete existing data from a database	
Organise and view data in different ways	
Share data using reports	

To sum it all up ...

- Most employers will expect their staff to be computer literate. If you've recently finished your education, you should have acquired basic computer skills.
- In terms of the workplace, you are most likely to encounter

word-processing/presentation software, spreadsheets and accounting software and databases. Although the system your employer uses may be different from the one you're used to, don't panic. If you are proficient in these areas using Microsoft or a similar popular package, you should be able to pick up a new system quickly.

- You should receive training in unfamiliar systems. Never be afraid to ask for help and never be tempted to lie about what you are capable of. Computers are relatively easy to use but they can be a nightmare if they go wrong.

- If you feel that your ICT skills aren't as good as they should be, look for local classes. This is a training area that the government supports, and you should be able to find tuition in your area.

7 Self-management

When you start work, you'll have to take on a lot of responsibility not only for the tasks you do but also in managing yourself. As you've already seen, attitude is important to employers; as well as wanting employees with good functional skills, they also need to know that you have the right personal skills.

Managing yourself so that you act responsibly and make a positive contribution to the business is incredibly important. Time management, the way you dress and present yourself, the manner in which you face challenges and ask for help are factors that will influence an employer in your favour if you get them right. Many of the issues that we address in

this chapter will seem like common sense – but you'd be surprised how many people get them wrong!

When you start work, you'll continually need to upgrade your skills. We're going to look at why this is important and how you can take charge of your own learning. We'll help you assess your skills on an ongoing basis and identify areas where you need to improve. Then we'll suggest ways in which you can get additional help and training if you need them.

But first, answer these questions and read the feedback. They highlight aspects of self-management that will help you to impress potential employers – and make you a valuable employee when you get that job!

Managing yourself

1. You have an interview in an unfamiliar part of town. How will you make sure that you get there on time?
   A. Use the maps app on your phone and set off, giving yourself an extra ten minutes in addition to the estimated journey time.
   B. Visit the premises the day before to check out exactly where it is and how long the journey takes.
   C. Ask a friend to drop you at the interview in their car.

2. You have too much to do. How will you prioritise your tasks and make the most effective use of your time?
   A. Do the easiest jobs first and get them out of the way.
   B. Do the hardest and most time-consuming tasks first then you can stop worrying about them.
   C. Work out what is most urgent and tackle that.

3. How will you dress for your interview?
   A. Smartly – clean clothes and shoes, not too much make-up and no visible tattoos or piercings.
   B. Like you normally do – your dress is an expression of your character.
   C. In a business suit.

4. Your supervisor explains a task that she wants you to complete but you don't fully understand the instructions. What do you do?
   A. Muddle through – it can't be that hard.
   B. Explain that you need to be absolutely sure what to do and ask her to go through the instructions again.
   C. Panic – then ask a colleague to show you what to do.

5. When you start work, how will you get to know your colleagues?
   A. Wait for them to approach you.
   B. With a joke – it's always good to make people laugh
   C. Smile, introduce yourself and explain that you're a bit nervous.

Feedback

1. **B** Visit the venue in advance so you know exactly where you're going. Both A and C are unreliable – the phone map may not show you where exactly where you have to go (for example, if your interview is in a hospital there could be multiple sites and entrances) and your friend may suddenly be unavailable!

2. **C** It's not a question of getting work 'out of the way' but of identifying what you need to do most urgently and doing that first. Learning to prioritise tasks is a key employability skill that involves evaluating how your work affects you and your colleagues. In business, time is money; time management is important and something that you may receive training in.

3. **A** Clean and smart – those are the factors that really count. Your clothes don't need to be new or fashionable but they should be spotless and neat. Your tattoos may be precious to you but research shows that they can put off employers. A business suit isn't really necessary unless it's something you wear often and feel comfortable in. If you're uncomfortable because of your clothes during an interview, you're not going to perform well.

4. **B** It's your supervisor's responsibility to show you, not your colleague's, so ask her to repeat the instructions.

Muddling through and/or panicking could lead to disaster.

5. **C** Overconfidence, loudness, silliness – none of these will be attractive to your colleagues. You're the newbie; it's up to you to fit in with the people who are already there. You'll do this best by showing a little humility, asking for help and encouraging your workmates to be tolerant and protective towards you until you find your feet.

This short quiz was a whistle-stop tour of some of the self-management dilemmas you could face. The important message that you should have gained from it is that when you leave school/college and go to work, you go from the top of the ladder to the bottom again. It's up to you to show willing and convince others that you are happy to learn from them and fit in.

In Chapter 9, you'll find out a lot more about self-management as you explore ways of communicating with your colleagues.

Talk to older people who've been working for a while and ask how they deal with self-management issues. You might not always agree with their advice but you could learn a lot about how businesses work and what is expected of good employees. You can also get help from websites – there's loads of information and advice at www.skillsyouneed.com. You can also use the skills health check on the Careers Service website at nationalcareersservice.direct.gov.uk; this is easy to use and will highlight areas that you need to work on.

Taking responsibility

When you leave school or college and start work you're going to have to take responsibility for your own development and learning. It's one of the hardest things you'll do because it involves breaking a lot of habits that you've acquired in your life so far. It is also one of the most important skills you need to acquire if you want to make a success of your career.

In school and college, the learning environment is fairly formal. Teachers teach, you learn. Even if your school encourages you to find out information for yourself, you'll still have guidance and help. There is always someone encouraging you and helping you to acquire the skills and knowledge that you need.

When you start work, you'll find that the situation is very different. There won't always be someone standing over you advising or telling you what to do. You'll be expected to take over a lot of the responsibility for your development. How you do this is what we're going to consider next.

First, however, let's think about how we learn.

How do we learn?

Think about your learning experiences. They haven't all taken place in a classroom under the supervision of trained teachers! Look at this list of activities and make a note of how you learnt to do each one. Who taught you? How were you taught?

	Who taught me?	How did I learn to do this?
Ride a bike		
Swim		
Play a sport		
Read		
Get dressed		
Use the text facility on your phone		
Multiplication and division		
Wash and dry dishes		
Drive a car		
Put on make-up/shave		
Cook		
Understand photosynthesis		
Read a map		
Clean your teeth		

Obviously there may be some things in this list that you can't (or choose not to!) do. The point of the exercise was to show that we learn different things in different ways from different people. We asked Evan, who is 16 years old, to work through the list and tell us what methods he'd used.

I wasn't aware of learning some of the things on this list like reading and cleaning my teeth, but I suppose at some point I must have been taught by my parents. They also taught me to wash dishes and cook, although it didn't feel like learning because we're all expected to help out at home and you suddenly realise you can do these things. It's interesting watching my baby sister learn because a lot of the time she just copies what she sees my mum do – she wants to do the same things and I suppose that's how she learns.

Multiplication and division and photosynthesis were topics we covered in school. The teacher told us about them, then we answered questions and did loads of worksheets until we understood the theory. Then we used the theory in practical situations – I remember in biology we carried out experiments to find out what happened if you deprived plants of light and oxygen.

I've also learnt some stuff from my friends – texting and shaving. My dad would have showed me how to shave but it was less embarrassing to talk to someone the same age about it. Texting was trial and error – none of us could be bothered to read any instructions so we just muddled through until we got the hang of it. It's one of those things that the more you do, the easier it gets. It was the same with riding a bike – you watch other people then you have a go yourself until you can do it. I'm keen on rugby and I think I'm a better than average player. The way I learnt the game was a combination of instruction from coaches and practice. The coaches are really strict. They give us lectures, make us do the same things over and over again, get us to watch other teams to observe how they play. Because rugby has a lot of fixed rules, you can't rely on practice alone – you have to master the basics.

Evan's experiences are common to most of us in that we've all had a lot of 'teachers' in our lives and a lot of learning environments. All of this teaching and learning that we experience throughout our lives is stored and used when we need it – and that includes when we start work. As we've continually pointed out in this book, you have already learnt a lot of skills that you'll find useful in your career. Also, ways of learning become hardwired into our brains so that we can acquire new knowledge and skills when we have to. Your ability to continue to learn and develop is a key factor of your employability.

How we actually learn something is a subject that has fascinated psychologists for years. There are hundreds – if not thousands – of books and research papers on the subject and this book isn't the place to go into an in-depth analysis. However, it will help if you understand some of the basics.

One of the most frequently referred to theories of learning is David Kolb's learning cycle. An American professor who specialises in educational theory, Kolb suggests through his research that most of us learn in four stages that form a continuous cycle.

1. Experience: we do something.
2. Reflection: we observe and think about what we've done.
3. Theorising: we draw conclusions from what we've done – in other words, we learn lessons from it that influence what we do next.
4. Applying and testing: we carry out our new learning.

Because this is a cycle, one stage leads into the next – and we don't all start at the same point!

Let's put this into familiar terms.

> You are learning to swim. You jump into the water. You go
> under the surface and immediately panic because you inhale
> water through your nose and mouth and think you're going to

drown. You come to the surface, feeling very uncomfortable. You think about what you have done. You know that you are panicking because you are uncomfortable, and you are uncomfortable because you've breathed in water through your open mouth and nose. If you could enter the water without getting water into your mouth and nose, you would not panic. You work out that the way to do this would be to ease yourself into the water slowly by climbing down the ladder into the pool, breathing in air then putting your head under the water. You test your theory and discover that it works; by preparing yourself to go underwater (entering slowly, holding your breath) you stop inhaling water and don't panic.

You can apply this learning cycle to almost everything you do – and it is particularly useful when you're acquiring new skills. Do something, think about why it succeeded or failed, learn from what you've done and 'fine-tune' your actions, then do it again!

Learning styles

We don't all move through these stages of learning in the same way though, because we all have different styles of learning. If you think about your friends, you're probably already aware of this. You may have friends who sail through their studies and seem to soak up knowledge without really trying. Then there are the friends who are thorough and painstaking and have to go over everything half a dozen times. And there are the friends who can read a set of instructions and immediately make sense of them, whilst other people struggle to understand the first sentence.

Exploring learning styles is fun as well as being informative. Many psychologists have worked in this area and produced tests to help people identify their preferred learning style. Two of the pioneers in this field are Peter Honey and Alan Mumford, who developed a system in the 1980s that is still used today.

They concluded that there are four distinct styles of learner.

1. **Activists:** these are doers; they learn by trying out new experiences. They tend to act now and think later!

2. **Reflectors:** these learners think before they act, watch other people, gather information and look at the big picture before they take any action.

3. **Theorists:** these learners want to know why things happen so they work out the theory that underpins something before they do it.

4. **Pragmatists:** these learners like to try out new ideas and experiment. They approach most tasks confidently because they know that they'll master them through a combination of theory and practice.

In the swimming pool:

- the activist runs straight to the edge of the pool and jumps in three times. On the third occasion she manages to keep her mouth shut and not to breathe in
- the reflector looks at other people who are getting into the water and realises that novice swimmers who ease themselves in don't get their heads wet until they want to
- the theorist works out that the shock of hitting water triggers an automatic reaction that makes us inhale and that's why we swallow water
- the pragmatist listens to the swimming instructor who tells him how to enter the water safely, then practises the technique until he's confident.

The secret to learning successfully is to identify what style of learning best suits you and to use it when you can. However, you need to recognise that your learning style is not fixed in stone; it will vary according to what you're learning and your immediate circumstances. So, although you may feel that you're an activist by nature, when you're at work you may need to modify your style and become more of a reflector so that you learn from other more experienced colleagues.

If you want to explore your own learning style, check out some of the sites on the internet by entering 'learning+styles+questionnaire' in your search engine. But at this time in your life, take the results with a pinch of salt! Your learning style and learning experiences are changing frequently at this stage of your development so don't be too heavily influenced by a single test or quiz!

Learning at work

When you're at school, the responsibility for your learning is shared between you and your teachers. Let's be honest; a lot of people believe that the responsibility for making them learn rests with the teachers and they do the absolute minimum when they are in class. The learning environment is structured; you have to acquire certain skills and knowledge at certain periods during your school career, and these skills and knowledge are tested at regular intervals to make sure you're on track.

Teaching you to do your job well and helping you to develop further skills will be high on your employer's list of priorities. An organisation needs well-trained staff in order to survive and prosper. But your training won't be your employer's most important priority – that will be providing the goods and services that customers want and making a profit.

For this reason, when you start work you're going to have to change your approach to learning. You won't have a battery of teachers standing over you. You're going to have to take responsibility for your own learning in a big way. This means:

- identifying what you can do
- identifying what you can't do
- getting help to acquire new skills and knowledge that you need to do your job now
- continually looking for opportunities to upgrade your skills and knowledge so that you can do your job in the future.

The last point is very important. We live in a fast-moving world and nobody can afford to stand still. Because of new technology, new customer demands and competition from other organisations you'll find that your working environment changes continually.

Here are some examples of how this works in practice. Gregor, 18, is a legal clerk.

> I used Microsoft Office at school and on my own laptop. When I started work I discovered that although my employer used Microsoft as well, it was a much later version and it took me ages to get my head around it.

Tom, 22, is a retail manager.

> I'd only been in my retail job for six months when the assistant manager left. I was asked if I wanted to apply for the vacancy but I was a bit daunted by what it involved – stock management, liaising with suppliers, dealing with customer complaints. I wanted the job but I wasn't sure I could do it.

Rachel, 24, is a senior stylist.

> I'm a hairdresser. Once I'd completed my training and apprenticeship, I thought that was it – but I was so wrong. I'm continually looking for courses about new techniques for cutting and colouring. If I don't keep up with these, then I'll go out of business. I've also had to be trained in handling substances that are hazardous to health – and health and safety regulations often change.

If you want to succeed in your job, you're going to have to keep up with changes and preferably always be one step ahead. That means embracing change. If your job demands that you learn new skills and go back to college on day release, see it as an opportunity to enhance your career – not a chore that you're being forced into.

What do you need to learn?

There are numerous ways in which you can carry out an analysis of your development and training needs – and you shouldn't have to do it all by yourself. Hopefully your employer will be able and willing to help. But you'll certainly make your own development more effective if you're willing to spend some time analysing your needs and looking at ways in which you'd like your career to develop.

Identifying what you can do

Here we will briefly introduce you to a commonly used tool for problem solving called a SWOT (strengths, weaknesses, opportunities and threats) analysis; we'll return to it in more detail in Chapter 8. This simple exercise enables you to identify the strengths, weaknesses, opportunities and threats that you are currently facing and to make decisions about what to do next.

You can use this useful tool when you're assessing what skills you already have and what you can already do competently.

Here's how it works in practice.

Kieran works for an estate agent in London. He is based in the office and acts as a negotiator, answering queries, passing on offers from buyers to sellers and carrying out administrative duties. He is keen to advance his career and knows that this is the field he wants to specialise in; one day he would like to run his own company.

Kieran carries out a SWOT analysis and identifies the following points.

Strengths

- Excellent customer-service skills – he's good with people and can talk easily to them.
- Good negotiating skills – he can get a deal that satisfies both sellers and buyers.
- Organised and conscientious – he enjoys the admin side of the job.
- Ambitious – he's willing to work hard to succeed.

Weaknesses

- He has no experience in anything except negotiating and customer service. To work his way up the career ladder, he needs to start valuing property.

Opportunities

- His boss has said that Kieran can come out with him sometimes on valuation trips.
- There are a lot of courses available in the area leading to relevant professional qualifications.
- London has a lot of agencies so Kieran can move around if necessary to improve his experience.

Threats

- Unstable housing market – will there always be a demand for estate agents?
- Reduced profits mean that there is less money in the company's training budget – will Kieran's boss be willing to pay for the courses that Kieran needs to go on?
- Lack of time. Kieran works long hours – can he find the time to study as well?

By writing down the results of his SWOT analysis, Kieran can get a clear picture of where he is now and how he can proceed: he needs to get experience in valuing property and start exploring professional qualifications. Obviously it doesn't give him all the answers but it does balance the positives and negatives.

Getting help

It's hard to make decisions about training and development alone and, luckily, most of us don't have to. Managers are trained to help their staff make decisions about their professional futures that will help both the individuals and the organisation. Your manager should be the first person you talk to about improving your skills and career development.

In large organisations, there will also be human-resources (HR) and training departments with dedicated staff who can advise and guide you. Don't be afraid to ask for help; it's not a sign of weakness but an indication that you're keen to make progress.

You can find out a lot about your training and development options by talking to colleagues, friends and family. How did they get where they are today? What advice can they offer?

Finally, if your employer doesn't offer training courses check out the local colleges and find out what is on offer. You can now study for many different professional qualifications in your own time, either at a night class or by distance learning. Yes, this demands dedication and you may have to burn the midnight oil, but it is a way to improve your skills base while you continue to work.

Learning opportunities

When you start work, you'll find that there are lots of different ways you can gain the new skills and knowledge that you need. Some of these will be familiar to you. For example, during your first few days in a new job you may have to complete an induction that involves sitting in a classroom and listening to someone tell you what you need to know!

Some of the methods will be new to you, so here's a quick rundown of the types of learning opportunity that may be accessible in your organisation.

- **Sitting by Nellie**: we have no idea who Nellie was but this is the term used to describe a learning situation where you work with someone more experienced and copy what they do until you are confident and proficient. It's a particularly useful method if you are learning mechanical or repetitive actions. 'Nellie' will show you what to do a number of times until you think you can do the task yourself. She will then supervise you while you practise.

- **Training courses and workshops**: you may be asked to take part in training courses at work or at training centres. These could be related directly to your job or to work in general – for example, you may be asked to attend a health and safety course. This type of learning opportunity usually demands time spent away from your job where you focus just on the training, so it's useful if you need to learn a new set of skills.
- **Work shadowing**: this is different from 'Sitting by Nellie' because it involves observing rather than doing a different job. You may have done this on work experience – you 'shadow' an experienced or more senior colleague to watch what they do and how they do it. This is a useful method if you're being promoted and want to see what your new role will involve.
- **Job rotation**: this involves doing someone else's job for a while. If you work in a sales office, you may be moved into complaint handling for a few weeks – and the complaint handler will be moved into your job. This is a good way to encourage staff to acquire new skills and broaden their horizons – and it helps organisations to develop a more versatile workforce.
- **Distance learning**: many organisations encourage their staff to acquire professional qualifications whilst they are working. One of the easiest ways to do this is to choose a distance-learning course where you study at home in your spare time using specially designed materials (both printed and computer-based). It gives you a chance to learn the theory that underpins the actual work you are doing.
- **Mentoring and coaching**: a mentor is an experienced member of staff who offers to guide you and 'show you the ropes'; this can be particularly useful when you start work because it gives you someone to turn to for advice. A coach will work with you on a one-to-one basis and show you how to do your job more efficiently and productively.

This is only a small sample of the learning opportunities that you may be able to access. Don't be afraid to talk to your manager about what you want to do, and ask for their advice. Generally enthusiasm is a quality that employers like to see!

Feedback and appraisals

Something you'll get a lot of at work is feedback. Feedback from your boss, from your colleagues, from your customers, from the press ...

Feedback is an essential part of the learning process. By getting feedback you'll learn what you're doing well and where you can improve. Feedback is not criticism; it should always focus on improvement, not on making you feel bad about your performance! Obviously there may be times when feedback focuses on things that you're not doing well – for example, if you are not getting to work on time, or you're handling customers badly. But hopefully the person that gives you feedback will also help you to improve.

Of course, you're already used to getting feedback from your teachers and lecturers. They, however, are trained to deliver opinions gently and to encourage you. Look at your end of year reports; you should find that they highlight what you can do well and where you should go next.

Not all managers are quite so proficient in delivering feedback and they might sometimes sound critical or impatient. Try to look beyond their manner and think about what they are saying to you. If they feel it is necessary to criticise there will usually be a good reason for this. Remember that your manager's focus is on making the business successful, not on protecting your feelings! So think about what you've been told and work out how you can improve. If timekeeping is your problem, make more of an effort to get up early. If you're not good at dealing with customers, watch how your colleagues do it and ask for more training. Just don't throw your toys out of your pram and sulk because someone has highlighted your imperfections.

Most companies review staff performance regularly through a system of appraisals. These are interviews with your manager that normally take place six-monthly or annually. Their purpose is to bring together your needs with those of your manager and the organisation as a whole. It's a chance to:

- review your performance over a given period of time, identify any problems and make sure that your career is on track
- plan your future development and look at how your career will move forward until the next appraisal. How will your job develop? What shape will your training take? This is your chance to highlight any skills gaps that you've identified or to tell your manager what you'd like to do.

A successful appraisal system will always be based on specific targets and objectives. To show what this means, read Maha's experiences with two different employers.

I'm a travel consultant. The first company I worked for wasn't very big – just three branches – and although I was told that I'd have an appraisal every six months, it was nearly a year after I'd started that my manager got round to it. It was a very informal chat – she checked that I wasn't experiencing any problems and suggested that I focus on a particular area of the business, and that was about it. To be honest I didn't have any complaints at the time about the process because I was too busy to think about it much.

When I went to work for a bigger and more structured organisation, the appraisals were very different. Shortly after I started work, I was interviewed by both my manager and someone from HR, and they were both very professional. We agreed a series of objectives that I would achieve before my appraisal in 12 months' time. I was asked to complete another sales training course and to spend a period shadowing a manager in another branch. We also set my sales target for the coming year. The advantage of working like this was that I knew exactly what was expected of me. The man from HR talked me through the various training opportunities and said he'd make sure that they were put in place.

At the end of the year, I had my appraisal interview and we were able to measure how much progress I'd made by assessing whether I'd met my targets. I said that I wanted to focus as much as possible on the cruise market because it was expanding, and my manager agreed that I could join the team that deals specifically with this area. We set more targets for the coming year. Although the process is pretty formal – everything is written down – I like the sense of purpose it gives me. I know what's expected of me.

Obviously the appraisal process isn't always as smooth as it was in Maha's experience. You may find that you don't get on too well with your manager, or you're afraid to voice your opinions. Some managers don't much like doing appraisals and see it as a waste of their time. But these are problems relating to individual people, not to the process itself. If you experience problems with your manager there should be someone else you could talk to (a mentor, another manager, someone in HR). If that isn't possible, try to understand where your manager is coming from and be patient. Remember that when people are abrupt or impatient, it is often because of their own problems rather than because of you!

To sum it all up ...

- Self-management is a key personal skill. Employers need you to recognise the importance of managing your time, presenting yourself well and working amicably with colleagues.
- Remember that you're the new member of staff and the onus is on you to fit in – not on everyone else to fit in with you!
- When you start work, you also start to take more responsibility for your own learning and development.
- There are development opportunities everywhere as long as you can identify them. Most employers will be pleased if you ask for extra training but it helps if you know what you want to do and why you want to do it.

■ Remember that you're an employee and any training and development you request should benefit the company. Your boss isn't going to pay for you to go on an expensive residential training course because she thinks you'll enjoy it. You need to show that by improving your performance you can improve the organisation's performance, too.

■ If you work for a small company where training budgets are limited, look for ways to learn from your colleagues and managers.Explorethepossibilitiesofacquiringnewskillsbywork shadowing, job rotation, etc.

■ Don't stop learning! The world never stands still and you can't afford to stand still either.

8 Thinking and solving problems

We think about and solve countless problems and make dozens of decisions every day – so many that often we don't notice them. Obviously many of these problems and decisions are minor and won't have a huge impact on our lives. Deciding what to wear, what to eat, what time to go out may seem important at the time but these decisions are hardly likely to change the course of world history.

There are, however, occasions when we have to solve problems and make decisions that are important and affect other people. In these situations, we need to think more carefully. Relying on 'gut instinct' and following a hunch isn't good enough; we have to weigh up the pros and cons before we decide on a course of action.

In this chapter, we're going to look at problem solving and decision making from a very logical angle. We'll show you how to approach problems and analyse evidence so that you can come up with appropriate solutions, and how to balance possibilities so that you make logical decisions. We'll also show you some simple techniques that will help you, even when you're under pressure. But first, let's consider the types of problems you have to solve and the decisions you have to make in your life now.

What's the problem?

Sometimes, life seems to be one long list of problems. From the minute we get up to the time we go back to sleep, we have to come up with solutions and make decisions. It's not surprising that by the end of the day we're exhausted. Solving problems and making decisions involves taking responsibility – and that can be very tiring!

The problems we're asked to solve and the decisions we have to make vary enormously from simple, fairly straightforward ones that won't have a major impact, to complicated ones that could affect our lives and the lives of the people we live and work with.

Here's an example of the dilemmas that Ali is currently facing. She's starting to feel inundated by problems and everyone is hassling her for decisions – so now she doesn't really know where to start.

Ali is 16 years old, and still at school. Since she got up this morning, she's been thinking about all of the following.

- Her A level choices – she has to decide what she wants to study next year and make a final decision by the end of the week.
- Her future career – she thought she wanted to become a teacher but isn't certain whether she has the right sort of personality for the job.
- Her boyfriend – they've been arguing a lot recently and she's not sure whether to finish with him.
- Her hair – should she get it cut short?

- Money – she wants to open a new bank account but isn't sure which bank offers the best deal.
- Her birthday at the end of the month – some of her friends have suggested they spend the day in London celebrating, but others want a party nearer home.
- School work – most of it is going well but she's having major problems completing part of her coursework because she's not sure she understands what she's supposed to do.
- Her weekend job in a local shop – should she pack it in now that school work is taking up so much of her time and focus on her studies?
- Lunch – pizza or a healthy salad?

As you read through this list of Ali's problems and the decisions she has to make, you can probably see that they vary enormously in terms of how serious they are. Her choice of A-levels could impact on her future studies and career; this is an issue with long-term implications. The haircut, however, may seem serious at the time (or if it goes wrong!) but hair eventually grows again and whatever Ali decides, it won't change the course of her future.

You may also have noticed that all these problems and decisions don't operate on the same time frame. The decision about A levels needs to be taken fairly quickly, as does the one about what to eat for lunch, but some of the others could wait. Ali doesn't need to decide on her future career at this very minute and she could put off making a decision about both the hair and the boyfriend for a while.

A third point is that, in many cases, if Ali is going to solve her problems and make the best decisions for her situation, she needs more information. Her problems with her coursework can't be solved without help from her teachers; to make a decision about a career in education she needs to know exactly what that would involve.

Urgent or serious: or both?

Look at the list of Ali's problems again and this time decide what you would put in the two columns on the right of the table.

In column 1, use the following scale to decide how urgently Ali needs to act.

> a = as quickly as possible
> b = fairly quickly
> c = the problem needs to be addressed but there's no urgency
> d = can be put on the back burner

In column 2, use the following scale to decide how serious the problem is.

> a = very serious, the decision could have long-term effects
> b = serious, but the decision could be reversed if necessary
> c = not too serious, the decision won't seriously affect other people or have long-term effects
> d = not at all serious, the decision won't make a difference to other people

Ali's problems	1 Urgency	2 Seriousness
Deciding on her A level choices		
Deciding on a future career		
Ditching her boyfriend		
Getting a new haircut		
Opening a bank account		
Making birthday arrangements		
Completing course work at school		
Whether to leave her weekend job		
What to eat for lunch		

By grading the problems/decisions, Ali is taking the first step towards getting a grip and sorting them out. Panicking and feeling overwhelmed isn't going to help her find solutions to her dilemmas; putting them in order and dealing with them in order of urgency and seriousness will make them more manageable. Any problem/decision that is graded a/a needs to be dealt with first – as quickly as possible!

Obviously this isn't an exact science and sometimes it's not easy to decide just how serious a problem really is. But it can help you to rationalise all that you have to think about – and that will help you to get a grip on your problems and decisions.

Now try it for yourself. Draw up a table like the one below. Write a list of the problems/decisions that you are currently thinking about, then grade them according to their seriousness and urgency.

My problems	1 Urgency	2 Seriousness

Your approach to problem solving

Let's consider how you approach problem solving and decision making.

Look at the statements in the box on the opposite page and give yourself a score using the following scale.

1 = always
2 = sometimes
3 = rarely
4 = never

Statements	Score
I decide what I'm going to wear the following day before I go to bed at night	
I like to have time to think over my options before I make a decision	
I collect information before I start to look for an answer to a problem	
I get irritated if I'm expected to make snap decisions	
Other people sometimes get annoyed because I don't give immediate answers	
Whenever possible, I consult with other people before I make a decision	
I avoid answering texts and emails immediately and wait until I've had time to think about them	
I set aside time at the end of the day to review what I've done and plan what I'll do tomorrow	
I write down the pros and cons of a situation before I make a decision	
I face problems head on – they're not going to disappear if I ignore them	

Now add up your score.

If your score is low (10–15) then you already take a fairly measured approach to problem solving and decision making. You like to plan ahead, weigh up the options and take time over your decisions. This may, however, make you unpopular with people who need a quick decision or who have a different approach.

If your score is high (25–40) then you probably 'think on your feet' and tend to solve problems and make decisions quickly. You may rely a lot on instinct; you know what feels right, and you base your decisions on those feelings. This isn't necessarily a bad thing, but it can sometimes be dangerous – your instincts won't always be right.

Most of us will score somewhere between these two extremes. That's because sometimes we use logic to solve problems and make decisions, and work through a proper process, but other times, particularly when we're in a hurry, we make snap decisions.

A logical approach

So, when you have a major problem to solve or an important decision to make, how should you approach it? Here's a suggestion for a logical approach.

- Analyse the problem. Write down on a piece of paper exactly what you need to do.
- Make sure you have all the information that you need. Don't jump to conclusions until you're sure you have all the facts.
- Consult other people who know something about the subject or will be affected by your decision. You don't have to take their advice but it may be worth listening to.
- Draw up a list of options.
- Make your decision.
- Put it into action.
- Review your decision once you've acted on it. Is it working out? Do you need to modify it?

Let's use this approach with Ali's decision about what subjects to study at A level.

	What Ali needs to think about/do
Analyse the problem	Why she's studying A levels – what does she want to get out of them?
	What's more important – choosing subjects she loves or ones that will be 'useful'?
	When does the decision have to be made by?
Gather information	What A level options are available in her school?
	If she doesn't like these options, where else can she study? How much work will be involved for each subject?
	What is in the syllabus for each subject – are there areas of study that she isn't happy about?
	What can she do if she makes a wrong choice and discovers that she doesn't like one of the courses?
Consult other people	What do her parents, teachers and friends think she should do? What do careers advisers suggest?
	How useful are her choices if she's aiming to get into university?

Draw up a list of options	Using all of the information and opinions she's gathered, she should identify at least two possible combinations of subjects that she could study.
Make a decision	Choose the most workable solution – the one that meets most of her needs.
Put it into action	Tell the decision to the people who need to know about it.
Review the decision	Keep monitoring her progress to make sure that the courses are good for her. If they're not, take action as quickly as possible.

Now try using this approach with one of your own problems/decisions and see if it helps you to sort through your options and make a choice. Again, you need to draw up a table like the one below in which to record your thoughts.

	What you need to think about/do
Analyse the problem	
Gather information	
Consult other people	
Draw up a list of options	
Make a decision	
Put it into action	
Review the decision	

Remember that this approach isn't foolproof and we don't always approach our problems and decisions logically. There will still be times when your heart rules your head. However, it's a good way to start.

Problem-solving techniques

So, how can you put this theory into practice and work through problems and make decisions logically?

When you know what your problem involves, you need to collect information so that you can weigh up your options. You'll already be used to doing this – a lot of your school or college work involves collecting information then evaluating it and deciding what to use and what to discard.

If you've ever carried out a scientific experiment, you'll know that there are certain principles that you must always apply.

- Don't rely on guesswork; base your experiment on factual information.
- Don't draw any conclusions until you've carried out the experiment and observed what happened.

The same principles apply to problem solving and decision making.

- Collect factual information: don't rely on rumour, gut feelings or guesswork.
- Don't anticipate the conclusion! That means trying to avoid having the 'right answer' in your head before you work through the problem. Keep your mind – and your options – open until you've evaluated all the information.

That's easy to say but how does it work when you're up against a major decision that needs to be made fairly quickly?

The answer is: very well, as long as you don't panic and make a rush decision and you use some tried and tested problem-solving tools to help you.

Have a look at Govindar's experiences when he was involved with helping to design a product he and his classmates had developed at college.

A group of us had designed a new type of insulated water bottle as part of our design and technology course. We'd made the prototype and we were really pleased with the way that it looked and worked but we had problems coming up with a name, deciding on the colour for the packaging and putting together some literature to promote it to customers.

Choosing a name was really difficult. One of the group wanted to call it Chill, but the rest of us weren't keen – but we didn't have any better ideas. At first it looked as if we'd have to go with Chill because we couldn't think of anything else, but then we decided to turn the naming and packaging exercise into a proper piece of market research and spend a bit of time on it.

We had a meeting where we brainstormed names, wrote down everything we could think of – and some of them were really stupid – then created a shortlist of the top five. We did the same thing with the packaging colours and one of the team drew up some basic designs. Then we went out and talked to 20 students (because students were the sort of people we thought would be interested in a product like this) and got them to vote for their favourites.

I was quite surprised by the final selection because it wasn't the one that had grabbed me. But one of the names won by a large margin and almost all the people we talked to chose the same packaging design, so we went with that.

Although it wasn't my choice, I was reassured because we'd worked through a logical process and come up with an answer that appealed to the majority. Because we'd done this market research to solve the name and design problems and reach a decision, I felt that we had less chance of going wrong.

You're probably already familiar with some problem-solving and decision-making tools, even if you don't realise it. Here are some of the simplest and most useful.

The Five Whys
Have you ever watched a small child drive its parents to distraction by asking why?

Dad, why is it raining?

Because it's cloudy today.

Why?

Because there's water in the sky.

Why?

Because the Earth is covered with water vapour.

Why?

I don't know! Eat your dinner!

The Five Whys tool is based on a similar principle: keep asking why until you get to the root of a problem. It also helps you to evaluate information and make sure that it is valid; it will show you (like Dad) where your information runs out and you're acting on guesswork. It's incredibly easy to use – so it can be employed quickly and applied to almost any problem.

You can apply this to any problem at work to help explore it in more detail.

Sorry, you can't take your holidays during the first two weeks of August. Why?

Because we don't have sufficient staff to cover that period. Why?

Because three other people have already booked those weeks off. Why?

Because they were asked for their holiday dates before you. Why?

Because they've worked here longer and we asked them first. Why?

Because it's the fairest way to decide on holiday dates. The longest serving staff members get first choice. But when they started here they were in your position and had to take whatever dates were left over!

See how the system works? This staff member still won't get the holiday dates she wanted but at least she now has factual information to help her understand why.

Brainstorming

Brainstorming has been around for more than 50 years. It's a technique that encourages people to think creatively about their problems rather than focusing on a narrow range of options. Because nobody is allowed to criticise other people's ideas, it encourages everybody to make suggestions and to contribute to problem solving and decision making.

You've almost certainly used this technique in school or college.

A group of you get together.

- One person is appointed the 'scribe' and writes down what the others say.
- The problem is written at the top of a large sheet of paper.
- For a fixed period of time (say 3–4 minutes) all of the group members call out any ideas that they have related to the problem.
- The ideas are written on the paper; they're not discussed or criticised.
- At the end of the period, the ideas are discussed and evaluated, and the best one(s) are selected.

Try this technique with a couple of friends. Discuss a problem that one of you is facing and see what happens. You should find that, although there may be no easy answer, you will widen the range of options you have!

SWOT

When managers and other staff at work have to make important decisions, they often find it useful to carry out a SWOT analysis. It's another simple but effective technique that you can apply to all sorts of different situations to help you weigh up your options and come to a sensible decision.

Although the term SWOT may be unfamiliar, you've almost certainly used this technique at school or college. Every time a lecturer or teacher has suggested that you make a note of the pros and cons of a situation before reaching a decision, you've been SWOTting.

SWOT stands for strengths, weaknesses, opportunities and threats. Put these headings into a grid like the one below, then think carefully about all the information you can include in each quadrant.

The great advantage of a SWOT analysis is that it gives you an overview of the advantages and disadvantages of a situation. It summarises the pros and cons so that you have a snapshot of where you are now and this gives you a basis for making a decision.

Strengths	Weaknesses
What are your strengths? What are you good at?	What are your weaknesses? In which areas do you need to improve?
Opportunities	**Threats**
What factors in the outside world could be good opportunities for you?	What factors in the outside world could prevent you from making progress?

Let's go back to Ali. If you remember, one problem she faced was making a decision about her future career. She thought that she might like to become a teacher but she's not sure whether she has the right qualities. If she carried out a SWOT analysis, her grid might look like this.

Strengths	Weaknesses
Believe that teachers do a good job. Usually calm under pressure. Good communicator. Good teamworker.	Have a bit of a temper. Can be impatient. Not very keen on paperwork.
Opportunities	**Threats**
Teachers are always needed. Excellent training schemes. Could specialise in a subject area that interests me and that I am good at. Good long-term career prospects.	High standard of applicants so may be hard to get in. May have to move away from home to train/work. Competition for jobs is fierce, so it may be hard to find my first job.

This analysis will help Ali to get her thoughts in order and identify actions she can take if she decides that a career as a teacher is what she wants.

For example, she can tackle some of her weaknesses (try to manage her temper better and improve her patience). She can also balance the opportunities and threats (which is most important, a good long-term career or staying close to home?).

The grid also highlights uncertainties that Ali can't resolve at the moment; in this case, she knows that she will face tough competition to find a job when she's finished her studies. Perhaps she needs to think about other career options as well, so that she can pursue an alternative route if she can't find a role in teaching.

Obviously this is only a brief outline of how a SWOT analysis works but it should give you some idea of how useful it can be. If Ali found that there were far more points in her weaknesses and threats quadrants than there were in the strengths and opportunities, this would suggest she needs to think again about her career choice.

Problem-solving skills at school/college

So far we've shown examples of three techniques that you can use to solve problems and make decisions. There are many, many more. Some are specific to business situations (there's a whole list at www.mindtools.com) but many are applicable to wider situations.

Although you may not be aware of it, you have been taught many problem-solving and decision-making techniques in order to help you solve problems at school and college. Think about situations that you've been in such as the following.

- Deciding on a topic for a project or an extended piece of work. Think about the process you went through in order to make your choice; it will almost certainly have involved collecting information about the various options and selecting the subject that offered you the most scope.
- Choosing what subjects to study at GCSE or AS level. To do this you will have had to balance a number of factors: your

personal preferences, what subjects are most appropriate for your future career, what subjects are available, the limitations of the timetable, etc.

Problems at work

Employers often ask for applicants with 'proven problem-solving skills'. They're not expecting to find a new recruit who has all the answers! What they are generally looking for is someone who:

- doesn't panic when they have a problem to solve or a decision to make
- is reliable in a crisis – they don't panic or throw a hissy fit
- can examine a problem and make a sensible decision
- takes appropriate action.

When you start work, you should receive a lot of support from your colleagues and your boss. This will help you to learn the ropes of the job and also to recognise and deal with minor problems that occur frequently.

Jon works in a sports-equipment shop. We asked him to make a list of the problems that he faces during an average week. This is what he said.

When I first started working here, even the smallest problem seemed huge because I was scared of making a mistake. After a few weeks, those problems became part of the routine and I dealt with them automatically: the computerised till going wrong; complaints about products; too many people wanting to be served at once; angry customers. Looking back, I can't believe that these things used to stress me. I learnt to handle problems like this by watching and listening to more experienced staff members.

Now that I'm managing the place, the problems and decisions are bigger: working out staff rotas and trying to keep everyone happy; choosing new stock and trying to work out what will sell next season; recruiting new staff. Obviously, the more experienced and more senior you are, the bigger the problems and the more impact your decisions have. But I apply the same principles that I used when I started work – take it steady, don't do anything on impulse and ask more experienced colleagues for help when I need it. As long as you stay calm and are willing to seek advice, you can't go far wrong.

To sum it all up ...

Problem solving and decision making are part of everyday life. We often work through these processes using our instincts and prior knowledge. When we are faced by more serious or urgent problems and decisions, however, it helps to take a logical and structured approach.

- Don't be overwhelmed by your problems and try to deal with them all at once. Work out which are the most urgent and serious.
- Don't be afraid to talk to people and seek their advice. Most people are happy to share their expertise and opinions and they may have good ideas to contribute.
- Collect all the evidence before you make any decisions. Working on instinct and doing what feels best isn't necessarily going to provide the ideal solution.
- Try out different problem-solving and decision-making techniques. If one technique isn't appropriate for a particular issue, try another.

9 Working together and communicating

Teamwork is a bit of a buzzword in the modern workplace. We're all expected to be 'team players'. When we apply for a job, we're often asked for 'proven teamworking skills'. If your boss says that you're an 'effective member of the team', that's high praise indeed.

So, why is it so important to be able to work with other people? Why do you need to be a good teamworker – and how can you improve your teamworking skills?

In this chapter we're going to consider your attitude towards working with others and how proficient a teamworker you already are. An essential part of working with others is being able to communicate with a wide range of people. You've already looked at using written language effectively. Now we're going to think about how you communicate verbally. Can you be assertive or persuasive when you need to be? Can you get your message across clearly to individuals and to groups? And are you a good listener – can you process what people are communicating to you effectively?

Let's start by focusing on your ability to work with others.

What is a team?

Think about your life at school and/or college. When have you had to work closely with other people? What teams have you already been a part of? For example, if you play a sport, you'll most likely be part of a team. Within your class or learning group, you may be part of a team that has a particular task to fulfil.

> On a separate piece of paper, make a note about what being part of that team means to you. How is it different from the other groups of people that you mix with on a regular basis?

You may have recognised that the difference between being part of a group and part of a team is that the team members are all working together towards a common purpose. If you're a member of a football team, you and your fellow players have a common goal (sorry!) – you want to beat the opposition. If you're part of a team that's raising money for charity, you're all working together to make as much money as you can. So, a team is a group of people with a common purpose that they can only achieve if they work together.

If you're used to working in teams, you'll know that the common purpose is the guiding force for the team members. It's what drives everything that they do.

The team members in an effective team:

- trust each other
- accept that the team is more important than the individual members
- communicate with each other – they say what they think and don't store up bad feeling
- are willing to include different types of people with different skills and experience
- establish rules for the team so that everyone knows what is expected of them
- understand that they won't always agree – but are committed to sorting out their differences so that the team can achieve its goals.

How do you feel about teamwork?

Whatever job you're thinking about doing, the chances are that you'll be part of a team. Very few of us work totally alone; we all rely on others to help us do our job.

Let's start with a short self-assessment test to find out how you feel about working in teams. Think about teams that you've been part of – these could be sports teams, project teams in class, fundraising teams for charity, etc.

Answer these questions by giving each statement a score:

2 = often
1 = sometimes
0 = rarely

Statement	Score
I've learnt new skills from other people when I've worked on teams	
I listen carefully to other people's opinions	
I like discussing possible ways of working with other people	
I can work well with a wide range of different people	

Statement	Score
I like to share responsibility when something goes well	
I like to share responsibility when something goes badly	
I respect other people's ideas	
I like to spend time planning before I take action	
I am aware of how other people are feeling	
I avoid arguments whenever possible	

My score is......................

If your score is 16 or above, you feel positive about working in teams. This suggests that you've enjoyed teamwork before and that you recognise that a team can achieve a lot if everyone is pulling together.

If your score is between 10 and 16, you're undecided about teamwork. Maybe you've found that some teams worked well but others have been a bit of nightmare because there was a lot of argument and conflict. You know that in principle a team can achieve a lot – but you're not sure they work well in practice.

If your score is below 10, then you're not too keen on working with teams. You prefer to work alone and to rely on yourself rather than other people. That's not necessarily a bad thing – we're all different and we all have different ways of working. But perhaps you need to think about teams and their function in more depth so that you feel more positive about them ...

Why is working as a team so important?
In most organisations, success depends on people working closely together. Individuals within departments rely on their immediate colleagues. The sales department relies on the logistics department to get deliveries out on time. The managing director relies on other directors to help decide future plans.

Because of this need to work together, when you go to work, you may find that you're part of a number of different teams. All of the teams will have something in common: they exist to help the organisation work efficiently, deliver what its customers need and make a profit.

Here's an example.

Jake works in a call centre selling mobile phone packages.

- He is part of a sales team that has a common goal: to sell as many products as possible and make money for the company.
- He is also a member of the training team that works with new recruits to help them improve their sales techniques – so that they can sell as many products as possible and make money for the company!
- His boss has asked him to join a project team that is looking at new products that the company could sell, so that it continues to expand – and sell as many products as possible and make money for the company!

All of these teams have different purposes but they are all working towards the same final goal, which is to keep the company successful so that everyone continues to have a well-paid job.

Working with other people isn't always easy. You probably know from teams that you've already been part of that team members don't always agree with, or like, each other. But there are benefits to working in a team.

- Team members can learn from each other.
- More hands make light work! Sharing ideas, responsibility and hard work means that more can be achieved.
- Because a team shares the work amongst its members, the work won't come to a stop if one person is away or drops out.

Working in a team is also good for you as an individual. Most of us like to have other people around us with whom we can share our successes and grumble about our problems. Being part of a team means that you're not on your own, feeling isolated.

Different people, different team roles

If working in a team is such a good thing – and most employers seem to place a lot of importance on members of staff being 'good team players' – then why is it often so hard?

Read this extract from an interview with Hassan. He is a trainee chef in a large hotel. All the catering staff are divided into teams and he has to spend time with each one during his training. Here he describes the problems he experienced when he joined the team that worked from 6a.m. to 2p.m. preparing breakfasts and lunches.

> It was a bit of a nightmare because everyone on the team had different ways of going about their job and different ideas about how we should work, so there was a lot of conflict.
>
> There were five of us, plus the chef – and he was very much the boss so gave orders rather than worked with the rest of us. One of the guys I worked with, Larry, was really temperamental – he had some good ideas but he sulked if we didn't accept them. Another one, Grego, was really slow. His work was good but he was so fussy that he took too long to get things done and that held the rest of us up. Kirsty was very controlling – she wanted us to work to a really rigid timetable and got annoyed if we didn't. Lexie was OK – she seemed fairly cheerful and never lost her temper and you could ask her to do anything.
>
> I just wanted everyone to pull together because the work was hard enough without a load of in-fighting. It's a shame everyone on the team wasn't like me or Lexie.

What Hassan is describing is a mix of different personalities – and this is something we encounter when we start working together on teams. Each team member actually has some strengths.

- Larry might be short-tempered but he has good ideas and a flair for his work – he could help to get the rest of the team fired up.
- Grego is not so much slow as thorough and this is a useful quality to balance out team members who are more concerned with the 'big picture'.
- Kirsty is controlling but that shows she is committed to getting the job done properly. She's the sort of team member who is very organised and makes sure that the work stays on track.

On a day-to-day basis, however, when all these characters are crammed together in a hot, steamy kitchen with a fierce chef overseeing them, it might be hard for Hassan to step back and appreciate the finer qualities of his team mates!

If you've worked in a team at school, college, as a volunteer or in a part-time job, you can probably sympathise with Hassan. Wouldn't working together be easier and more effective if everyone had the same attitudes – in fact, if everyone was like you?

Well actually no, it wouldn't. A good team is made up of a balance of different people who all have different strengths. If everyone was the same, then the team would only be effective in a limited way.

Think about it this way: if a team was made up of six dynamic people who were full of good ideas but hated dealing with routine work and were hopeless at attending to detail, would anything ever get done?

Probably not.

A British management expert, Dr Meredith Belbin, studied the way that teams work together and suggested that the effective ones are made up of different types of people who will take on nine different roles.

The first three are **action-oriented** roles – these are the people that get things done!

Shapers	Outgoing people who like to make things happen, get excited by challenges and like tackling problems. Shapers can be argumentative and a bit too forceful so they offend other team members! In Hassan's team, Larry appears to be a 'shaper'.
Implementers	These are the people who turn ideas into action. Usually efficient and organised – but they may not like change and can be a bit fixed in their ideas. Kirsty seems to be the implementer in Hassan's team.
Completer-finishers	These people are thorough, pay attention to detail and like things to be done properly. They can be perfectionists though, which makes them hard to work with – and they don't always trust other people to do a job as well as they can! This is Grego in Hassan's team.

The second three are **people-oriented** roles – these are the team members that 'glue' the rest of the team together.

Coordinators	These are the team leaders and they are good at guiding other people. They tend to be good listeners, calm and easy-going so other team members get on well with them. On the down side, they may rely too much on other people.
Teamworkers	These people provide support to the team and make sure everyone works together. They are usually popular, good at recognising other people's strengths and very committed to making the team work well. They can be too 'nice', though – they don't like arguments or conflict and may not like making decisions. This is Lexie in Hassan's team.
Resource investigators	Popular, persuasive, good at building up contacts both inside and outside the team, their main strength is in pulling together all the resources so that the job gets done. They may lose their enthusiasm quickly, however, if things don't go smoothly.

The remaining three roles are **thought-oriented** – these are the 'ideas' people.

Plants	Good at developing new ideas and approaches to problems. Plants may not get on well with other people and prefer to work apart from the team – and they can sulk if their ideas aren't accepted. This role could be applied to Larry.
Monitor-evaluators	Smart, objective, good at analysing ideas and deciding what will work in practice. This can, however, sometimes make them seem negative about new ideas.
Specialists	These people have special knowledge that the team needs to achieve its goals – they are the experts. That can make them hard to work with because they are concerned with practical and technical issues. Grego is thorough in his work, so this role could also be applied to him.

You can find some examples of team role questionnaires on the internet to help you assess your own style. Treat these with caution. The most reputable, such as those administered by Belbin, need to be administered by professionals and paid for. Many of the others are interesting but not to be taken too seriously. Like all self-assessment tests, they rely on your answers and these can change from day to day. But if you're interested in finding out about your team-player qualities, try typing 'what+type+of+team+player+are+you+quiz' into Google.

How can you become a better member of a team?

Let's start with another quiz. Look at this scenario and choose the answers to the questions that most closely reflect what you would do. Be honest! Then think about the questions again and write down the answer that would be best for the team.

You've been elected to the committee of your college council. There are 10 elected members on the committee; two of them are good friends of yours, you know three of them quite well – and the remaining four are strangers. The committee has a lot of work to get through in the coming months. Meetings are held once every two weeks, on Thursday lunchtimes. Extra meetings are called when necessary and these usually take place after college hours.

1. Thursday lunchtime meetings are not good for you – that's the day when you finish college early and you usually go into town to meet up with your friends. Would you:
   A. try to persuade the committee to change the meeting time to another day?
   B. accept that you'll have to give up your social life on the days when there's a meeting?
   C. say nothing but miss some of the meetings?

2. Every committee member has to take on some administrative duties. You're not keen – you have enough work to do without taking on extra responsibilities. Would you:

A. keep quiet and hope that you're overlooked when the work is handed out?

B. tell the other committee members that you can't help because you're too busy?

C. volunteer for a role that you know you can handle fairly easily?

3. The committee is electing a chairperson and one of your friends has been nominated. You know she's a bit flaky at times and you're not convinced she'd be good at the job. Would you:

A. vote for her anyway, because she's your friend?

B. vote for the person you think is best for the job?

C. refuse to vote, because you don't want to choose the wrong person?

4. You get annoyed at meetings because the committee is slow at making decisions. Do you:

A. accept that everyone has a right to voice their opinions so it will take time for decisions to be agreed?

B. try to move things on by interrupting and showing your impatience?

C. use the time during meetings to catch up with your texting?

5. There's one person on the committee who really annoys you – he's arrogant, snobbish and never shuts up during meetings. Do you:

A. start a whispering campaign among the other committee members to get rid of him?

B. accept that we're all different and put up with him?

C. argue with him in meetings – hopefully he'll learn to keep his mouth shut?

6. You've been asked to give a presentation to the committee about the need for better sports facilities in college but you haven't got time to prepare properly. Would you:

A. ask someone else to do the job?

B. ask someone to help you?

C. 'get sick' and miss the meeting when you're supposed to give your presentation?

7. You often get very frustrated because answers to problems are so obvious but other committee members want to discuss everything in detail. Do you:

A. tell the other members that your suggestions make sense and save time?

B. suggest that a process is put in place to speed up decision making, such as time limits for discussions?

C. accept that a lot of time is wasted at meetings – and the committee often gets things wrong?

8. You were asked to circulate a set of papers by email before the committee meeting, but you forgot. Would you:

A. confess and apologise?

B. insist that you sent them out, and that it must have been a computer glitch?

C. 'get sick' and miss the meeting?

Now check your answers.

Obviously we don't know what your honest reaction to these scenarios would be but, you can compare them with the responses that a good teamworker would make.

1. **B** Good teamworkers accept that they'll have to make compromises when they work as part of a team. You might not like going to meetings on Thursdays, but if this is the best time for all the other team members, you'll have to accept it and reorganise your social life.

2. **C** Working in a team carries responsibilities so expect extra work. If you don't take on your fair share, you won't help the team achieve its goals – and you won't be popular with

your team mates. Volunteer for jobs that you can tackle confidently – or at least willingly.

3. **B** Obviously you feel loyalty to your friend but you won't be doing that friend or the team as a whole any favours if you put them in a role that they can't handle. The team has to come first, so vote for the person who is best for the job.

4. **A** Remember what you've already learnt about the different types of people that make up a team. Not everyone will think like you do, or act in the way that you think they should, but every team member is entitled to contribute their opinions. Be patient and listen to them – you might learn something.

5. **B** As with the previous question, this is a situation in which you need to show tolerance. Dividing team members by talking behind their backs is never a good idea and will backfire on you when inevitably you are found out. Similarly, arguing will only cause bad feeling within the team and could earn you a reputation as a troublemaker. Keep your feelings to yourself and focus on what the team has to achieve.

6. **A or B** Ideally you'd never get into this situation – if you've accepted a task then you have a responsibility to fulfil it. But if you find that, for a good reason, you can't carry out the presentation then ask someone else to do it or to help you prepare for it – and make sure you explain what happened to the rest of the team and acknowledge how others have helped you.

7. **B** There are solutions to most problems and a good team will work together to find them. You've got to respect the other team members and let them have their say. You also need to accept that team meetings sometimes seem rather slow to come to decisions. So look for ways to get round the difficulty of meetings dragging on – maybe set a time limit for discussing each item on your agenda, make sure only one person speaks at one time, and above all, appoint a good chairperson who can take charge of meetings and keep them moving. (Maybe this should be you!)

8. **A** Confess and apologise if you ever fall behind on your team duties or make a mistake. Most people are quick to forgive errors – we're all human. But lying or being cowardly don't go down so well. And in future, make sure you fulfil your commitments.

More about communication ...

In Chapter 5 we discussed the importance of accurate communication, particularly in writing. Now we're going to focus on other aspects of communication that are important when you're working with colleagues: speaking, listening and body language.

The communication cycle

The key to communicating verbally is understanding that communication is a two-way process. It involves both giving and receiving messages. Here's a simple explanation of how it works.

Person A has a message to communicate to Person B.

Person A communicates that message by encoding it (speaking it).

Person B receives the message and decodes it (listens to it).

Person B sends feedback to Person A to show that the message has been received and understood (nods, says 'uh-huh', sends a written acknowledgement).

So far, so simple. But, as we know, communication often goes wrong. That's because the message gets distorted. Think of the message like a radio programme that you're listening to when the signal suddenly weakens or is lost; you can hear bits of the programme but it's fuzzy and unclear. This is what sometimes happens during the communication cycle.

We call these distortions 'barriers to communication'. They are something you experience every day.

Think about this scenario. How many barriers to communication can you identify?

> *You're sitting in a lecture theatre listening to your tutor give a talk about global warming. There are 50 people around you and some of them are shuffling, reaching into their bags, flicking through notebooks. Somebody's mobile phone rings, which annoys the tutor and makes the rest of you laugh. A siren can be heard outside. The tutor has a flat monotonous voice and, to be honest, you're not all that interested in global warming at the moment. Added to which, you don't understand what she's saying because she seems to assume you have a lot of background knowledge about the subject. You're more concerned about the row you had with your brother last night about who can have the car tonight – it's your turn but he's insisting that his need is more urgent. At the end of the lecture you suddenly realise that you can't recall a single thing your tutor said.*

You probably recognised that some of these barriers to communication were external: the noise and movement of other people, the interruption caused by the mobile phone and the laughter and the tutor's boring voice. These barriers distract us from what we should be focusing on.

Noise is something we live with all the time – the sound of other people speaking, telephones ringing, traffic, music and televisions in the background, etc. We filter out a lot of this unimportant noise; if we didn't, our brain would rapidly become overloaded with the thousands of messages it was trying to deal with. The trouble is that sometimes our noise filters are too efficient and we forget to turn them off when we should. So, in the scenario that you've just considered, there's a risk that as well as filtering out the distracting background noise you might also filter out the words that you should be listening to!

The tutor's voice is another barrier; because it lacks variety and we find it boring to listen to, we find it hard to remain focused on the words and to listen properly to what is being said.

The other barriers – and the ones that are most likely to stop us getting a message clearly – are:

- lack of background information
- lack of interest in the subject
- your state of mind (being distracted by your own thoughts).

If somebody talks to you using words that you don't understand, or assumes that you already possess knowledge and information that you don't have, it is rather like listening to them speak in a foreign language. Because you're trying to decipher individual words and phrases you won't be able to focus on the whole speech and you'll quickly lose the plot. In a situation like this, if possible, it's essential to ask questions and ask for clarification as quickly as possible.

Being distracted is a common problem and happens when we focus more on our internal dialogues than on what is happening around us. Think about all the times when you've been listening or conversing with someone and you're actually talking to yourself inside your head!

I bet the next thing she says is about carbon footprints ... it is so cold in here ... I'm not sure anyone really changes their holiday plans because they might damage the environment ... that is a truly awful shirt she's wearing, why on earth did she choose a colour like that? ... Maybe if I just take the car before my brother gets home he'll get the message ...

Internal dialogues can be stimulated by all sorts of situations such as:

- physical distractions or discomfort
- something the person that you're listening to says that triggers off a reaction in your brain
- thinking you know what the other person is going to say.

Whatever the cause, the end result is the same: lack of concentration that means that the communication process is distorted and messages are not processed properly.

Listening and speaking

To receive a message, you really have to listen to it and that means getting rid of these distortions. It's not always easy but here are some tips to help you receive and decode messages accurately.

- Focus on what is being said. Look at the speaker. Don't look at your papers, mobile phone or anything else.
- If you feel your attention wandering find a way of reminding yourself that you should be listening: some people pull their ear lobes or kick themselves (gently!) to refocus. Any small movement is fine.
- Remove as many external barriers as you can – if the room is noisy, suggest moving. If you can't hear a phone call clearly, suggest calling back later.
- If there are interruptions, ask the speaker to recap on what they were saying when the interruption started.

You can't do much about the other person's boring voice but if you're aware of how distracting this can be, it will help you make your own speech more interesting! Here are some tips for giving a message so that it can be easily decoded.

- If possible, think about what you want to say beforehand and prepare. That doesn't mean writing a speech, but it does mean organising your thoughts.
- Think about your tone of voice – is it friendly or abrupt? If you speak in a harsh tone of voice, you may offend your listeners.
- Think about the speed at which you speak. If it's too fast, your listeners will lose track of what you're saying. If it's too slow, they'll go to sleep.
- Try to vary the tone and pace when you speak. Any lengthy speech, however interesting, can be boring if it's delivered in a monotone.

These are only a few suggestions. Start looking carefully at people who you think communicate well; look, for example, at hosts on TV chat shows. What makes them easy to listen to and understand? What techniques do they use that you could try? You'll probably notice that the key to their skills is the way that they focus closely on the person or people they're with. You can see it in everything they do, including their body language.

Which brings us on to the next section ...

Body language

... or, to give it its more accurate name, non-verbal communication signals!

Most of us are aware that our bodies talk – there was even a song about it. What we might not be aware of is just how much our movements and physical manner tell other people about what we are thinking and feeling.

It has been estimated that the human body is capable of more than 270,000 gestures, all of which mean something. When you're communicating with someone, more than half of your message is conveyed through your body language – your stance, facial expression, gestures, etc. Some of this will be deliberate, such as nodding to show that you understand something you've heard. However, a lot of your body language is subconscious, so you won't be aware that you're making the signals.

Now, this is a tricky area to deal with. There's such a lot of talk about non-verbal signals in the media that many of us believe that we're experts in the subject. We think we can interpret every gesture, movement and tone of voice. Most of us can't; it takes a real expert to accurately decipher body language. We also think that we can control our own body language and thus hide our real feelings. Again, most of us can't do this because our subconscious is simply too powerful. So, when you investigate non-verbal communication, be aware that a little knowledge can be a dangerous thing, as this scenario shows.

A man walks into a room and looks around vaguely. He sits hesitantly on the edge of the chair and can't relax. He doesn't look directly at the woman interviewing him, but stares at the floor. His hands are clenched in his lap, except when he touches the side of his face, which he does frequently. He is beginning to perspire.

'Hmmm,' the interviewer thinks. 'We've got a right one here. Why is he so uncomfortable? What is he hiding?'

'Oh no,' the man thinks. 'My contact lens has slipped and I think it's stuck in the corner of my eye.'

Obviously, the best course of action in a situation like this would be for the interviewee to explain his problem straight away so that the interviewer understands why he is so uncomfortable. Unfortunately, particularly in unfamiliar or stressful situations, we don't always take the best course of action.

Body language can easily be misunderstood but understanding the basic principles can help all of us to communicate better. Just remember that it is only one component of communication and must be considered alongside the words that are being spoken, tone of voice, etc.

The signals that you're most likely to be aware of are eye contact, posture and gestures. Let's look at each of these in turn.

Eye contact

This term is misleading – if we all walked around locked into the eyes of the people around us the world would be a truly spooky place. What we're referring to here is focusing on the person to whom we are speaking. Eye movements are extremely powerful because your eyes actually change according to what you are feeling.

- 'Wide-eyed' is an accurate description of what happens when you're interested in something or someone – your pupils dilate and get bigger.

- When you're distracted, your pupils contract and get smaller.
- Letting your eyes wander around a room suggests that you could be bored.
- Refusing to meet another person's eyes may mean that you have something to hide.

The general principle when you're communicating with someone is to make regular eye contact with them to show that you're taking an interest and paying attention. This has the spin-off benefit that it will actually help you to focus mentally and you will pay more attention. Avoid staring, though, as that can appear intimidating and aggressive.

Posture

Some of us naturally walk tall, some of us are slouchers – but we all use our posture in subtle ways to convey messages.

Think about how you stand and sit in these situations. Make notes on a separate piece of paper of two or three things that you do.

Take a look at your posture

When you're trying to make another person take note of you	
1.	
2.	
3.	
When you're defensive or afraid	
1.	
2.	
3.	
When you're confident	
1.	
2.	
3.	

We can't predict what answers you came up with but here are some general principles.

- When we want someone to take notice of us, we will hold ourselves more erect and make our bodies look taller and bigger. This might involve pushing back our shoulders and raising our chin if we are standing, and leaning forward if we're sitting down.
- Conversely, when we're afraid or defensive we'll withdraw and make our bodies small. We might hunch into a chair, slump our shoulders if we are standing, and cross our arms to protect our vital internal organs.
- If we're feeling confident, our stance will be relaxed and may be more expansive – shoulders back, making arm movements, legs akimbo, etc. Because we feel safe, we open up the front of our body towards the person we're talking to.

Even if what you do is different, the point is that your mood is reflected very clearly in the different postures you assume – and other people will recognise this. So though you may say out loud, 'Yes, that's great, I'm really happy for you,' if your hands are on your hips and your chest is thrown forward as if you want a fight, nobody will believe you!

Gestures

Tapping your fingers, pulling on a strand of hair, picking at that hangnail on the side of your thumb – these are tiny gestures that, in the grand scheme of life, probably seem unimportant. Like posture and eye contact, however, they give off signals to other people about what we're feeling.

Gestures are difficult to control because they are habits that have become deeply ingrained so we don't notice we're doing them. Cracking your knuckles, fiddling with buttons/pencils/your watch strap, waving your hands around when you're talking – you do these things without thinking about them. They can, however, be extremely irritating to the people you're with and they can signal a range of negative emotions like boredom, irritation and nervousness.

Obviously not all gestures fall into this category. We also use gestures to reinforce what we're saying: pointing, counting on our fingers, and opening our hands wide to show honesty are just three examples.

Don't get obsessive about trying to control your gestures; if you do, you'll end up in a locked room refusing to speak or move! Just try to be aware in important situations that you need to keep a focus on the person you're with and to show them that you are paying attention. And do be aware of any particular habits that you have that could irritate the people you're talking to – poking your ears and nose during an interview is not a good idea (and yes, it does happen!).

Using your communication skills at work

So far, you've had a brief introduction to the basics of communication. Now let's put this knowledge into a more practical context and look at how people use their communication skills in the workplace. We're going to focus on three particular situations because they are ones that might come up when you're looking for a job and when you first start work. The good news is that although you may not immediately make the connection, these are all situations that you're already familiar with from school, college and everyday life.

Asking and answering questions

We've been asking and answering questions since we learnt to talk. Strange, then, that so many of us don't understand how to do it in such a way that we get (or give) the right information.

When you're in education, your teachers have the skills to get information out of you. Those skills come with years of practice. At work, you may not be so lucky; you may be talking to people who are not naturally good communicators and who struggle to manage conversations and make them productive.

The key to asking and answering questions well is to understand that there are different types of questions, all of which have a different purpose. Here are the most commonly used types.

Question type	What they are for	Example
Closed questions	To get specific information and clarify facts	*Do you ...? Can you ...? How long ...?* Closed questions often only need a one-word answer – they don't encourage lengthy replies.
Open questions	To encourage someone to 'open up' and give a detailed reply	*Why did you do that? How did you feel when that happened? What happened afterwards?* Open questions need a more detailed response. These are the most frequently used questions.
Probing questions	To 'fill in the gaps' and get more detail about why you did/thought something	*You say that you're unhappy with the shop layout. Why is that?* Probing questions go beneath the surface. The questioner is genuinely curious about why something happened and isn't being critical.
Hypothetical questions	To find out what you would do in a particular situation	*If you were moved to another team and you didn't get on with your manager, what would you do?* Hypothetical questions are about something that might happen. They are designed to find out your opinioins/thoughts.

Don't stress about these question types; most of you will be using them all the time in conversation without thinking about them. What is important is that you're aware that there are different ways of getting the information you need, depending on your situation.

There are two other types of question that can cause problems.

1. Multiple questions, where you ask (or are asked) too many things at once, can be confusing. *So how long have you been in this department? Have you enjoyed it? How do you get on with the other staff?* Which part of the question should you answer first? Can you remember everything that's been asked? And will the questioner remember what you say? In

this situation you should deal with one question at a time, and don't be afraid to ask the interviewer for clarification.

2. Leading questions, where the questioner suggests the answer they want to hear! *You'll have to work alternate weekends. That won't be a problem, will it?* The way the question has been asked suggests that you have to agree that it won't be a problem – even if it is. Be wary about asking leading questions because you probably won't get an honest answer. If you're asked a leading question, you don't have to agree – but try to be tactful if you disagree. And never, ever respond to a leading question that asks you to comment on somebody else's shortcomings. *If you're asked: What do you think about xxxx? She's a bit of pain, isn't she?* don't be tempted to agree, even if you think it's true. You can guarantee that if you're rude about a work colleague, they'll eventually find out about it.

Receiving and giving instructions

You might think that to date your life has been nothing but receiving instructions. 'Clean your room', 'Finish that piece of work', 'Get off the phone' ... somebody somewhere is always telling you what to do.

The difference when you start work is that you will have less scope to ignore instructions or to negotiate what you have to do. When your boss says, 'Take those papers through to the accounts department', you're not in a position to:

- ignore him/her
- say, 'Yeah, when I'm ready'
- ask, 'Why?'

Unless you're being asked to do something that appears dangerous or downright stupid, you receive the instruction and you fulfil it. There are two reasons for this.

1. It's your boss's job to tell you what to do and it's your job to do it.

2. Unless you're working for someone who takes pleasure from making you do unnecessary tasks, there will usually be a good reason why you're being instructed to do something.

Your boss is asking you to take the papers to accounts because it's a job that contributes to the smooth running of the organisation, which contributes to customers' needs and wishes being fulfilled, which contributes to the organisation making money and you being paid at the end of the month.

It's essential that you receive instructions accurately so that you do what is expected. Sounds easy, but the process does involve a number of stages:

- receiving the instructions
- clarifying the instructions to make sure you've understood what is said
- giving feedback so that the person giving the instructions knows that you've understood and will act appropriately.

In many cases you'll do this automatically without thinking about it but sometimes the situation will be more complicated because of the way in which the instructions are given. Look at what happened to William.

I was working in a warehouse. I'd been through an induction course and learnt the basics of how the place operated and the manager had appointed a 'buddy' to work with me and show me the ropes. For the first couple of weeks it was fine. Then one day my buddy wasn't in and one of the foremen that I didn't know rushed in and said we needed to send an urgent order out, gave me the order sheet and rushed off again. I wasn't sure what to do but there wasn't anyone around to ask and I didn't want to bother my busy manager. So I sorted out the parts, packed them up, labelled the box and sent it down to despatch. I didn't think about it again – other than congratulating myself for dealing with the emergency – until a couple of days later when I got a real telling off. The order form was handwritten, I'd misread the part number and sent off the wrong pieces. The customer was furious because my mistake had held up their production line.

William faced two problems.

1. The foreman gave the instructions badly. He didn't check that William had understood or wait for feedback to make sure that his instructions would be carried out correctly.
2. William didn't have the confidence to find the foreman and ask for clarification or to ask his manager for help.

Not every situation like this can be avoided, but there are some things that you can do to make your life easier when you're asked to do something.

- Remember the old adage that 'more haste means less speed'. It's better to take a little time to clarify instructions than to rush into a job and get it wrong.
- Asking for instructions to be repeated or clarified doesn't reflect badly on you. It's better that you admit you don't know what to do than make a mistake. Everybody has to learn and questioning is part of that learning process.
- Feedback is an essential part of the process. When someone gives you an instruction, repeat back what they want you to do to make sure you've got it right.
- If you show that you are willing and eager to carry out the instructions, that makes up for a lot of questions! It's your attitude that counts.

Speaking to a group of people

Not many years ago, the only people who gave presentations seemed to be senior managers and professional speakers. Now, everybody seems to be expected to make them. It's something that, increasingly, you're expected to do in school and college. At the very least this involves standing up and talking about your project to a group of people in class, which many of us find difficult and embarrassing.

When you start work, you may be involved in presentations with your colleagues – for example, telling a group of managers how your part of the business is performing. Alternatively, you may be asked to give a presentation yourself if you've been working on a particular project.

If you don't like speaking out, then giving a presentation to people you don't know well (for example, during a school function) can be an intimidating prospect. But it has to be done and there are ways to make the process less stressful.

- Planning, planning and more planning. Think about what you want to say, make notes, then put your thoughts in order. Do this well in advance so that you have plenty of time to complete your preparation.
- Make notes – but try not to make a prepared speech. If you read a speech or memorise what you plan to say and then recite it, your delivery may be flat and boring for your audience.
- Think about how you're going to start your presentation – what will grab your audience's attention? You don't need to do handstands but if you start off sounding bored, then you'll put your audience to sleep.
- Use visual aids such as PowerPoint slides, but only if they support what you have to say. Don't get so carried away with the technology that it takes over from the substance of your presentation.
- Keep it short and simple (KISS). Stick to the point, tell your audience what you're going to say, say it, then tell them what you've said. This gives them a chance to absorb your words.
- Use body language to connect with the audience: smile at them, look directly at them and use gestures if they're appropriate.
- If you're part of a group of people who are giving a presentation, don't try to take over. This is a team effort; it's not all about you! Take a deep breath before you start, make sure everyone is looking at you, greet them – and remember that most (if not all) of the members of the audience are on your side and want to hear what you have to say.

What Employers Want

Here, Katya talks about her experience of giving presentations in her job.

I'm a beautician, working in a spa in a fairly large hotel. The last thing I expected to have to do is to stand up in front of my colleagues and give them a talk about new methods of exfoliating skin! But presentations are one of the ways in which we pass on our knowledge to our colleagues so it had to be done.

The system works like this: if any of us go on a training course for a new product or technique, we're expected to share what we've learnt during our Monday morning staff briefings. Every Monday morning the spa is closed until lunchtime so that all of the staff can get together. Each week, someone will give a presentation to the rest of us. That means that we're all familiar with all the treatments that the spa can offer, not just the ones that are relevant to our own section of the business. So, for example, I know what the manicurists do, I understand the latest massage therapies, etc. and I can recommend these to my clients.

The first time I stood up to give a presentation I was really nervous even though it was to people that I knew well. I know that it probably wasn't very good – I talked for too long, and I kept stumbling and forgetting what I wanted to say. Added to which, I was just talking and my audience got bored pretty quickly.

Since then, I've improved a lot. One trick I've learnt is to show instead of just telling. I demonstrate techniques on other members of the team. If I have free samples, I give them out and show how to use them. There are always lots of promotional leaflets from the manufacturers so I give those out too.

I know that my audience are genuinely interested in what I'm saying because I can see it on their faces and they always ask questions. I enjoy giving the presentations now that I've gained confidence, so much so that I think I might take a teaching qualification so that I could teach beauty therapy at night school.

Katya's experience is a common one and worth remembering: the more presentations you give and the greater your creativity in your presentation, the easier the process becomes.

To sum it all up ...

In this chapter, you've learnt a lot about working in teams and communicating verbally with colleagues. The key points are as follows.

- A team is a group of people who have a common purpose.
- Working in teams can benefit an organisation by encouraging people to work together to solve problems. It can benefit you because you'll learn from your team mates.
- Teams that work well together can achieve more than individuals working on their own.
- Teams are made up of different types of people – and this is a good thing.
- You might not be a committed team player – but you can still improve your team skills.
- We communicate with other people all the time, both consciously (through the words we speak) and subconsciously (through our non-verbal communication skills).
- The way that we communicate influences how other people think about us.
- Think before you speak. This helps you to avoid 'putting your foot in it' and to choose appropriate words and body language.
- Remember that communication is a skill and, like every skill, you can work to improve your command of it. Don't try to hide behind statements like, 'I'm not good with other people,' or 'I'm not good at making myself clear.' We all have the capacity to be good communicators if we give ourselves the chance.

10 Understanding the business

Nobody works in a bubble. What you do impacts on your colleagues, managers, company owners and customers. In this chapter, we explore why it's important to look at the big picture and to learn as much as you can about the organisation you want to work for. How does your job fit into the whole? What are stakeholders and how do they influence what you do at work? And, when you understand the business you're in, how can you contribute to it most effectively?

One of the personal skills that the UKCES believes almost everyone needs to do almost every job is understanding the business. This may seem strange if you're looking for your first job. Surely understanding the business is something that comes with time once you are actually in a job? How can you be expected to understand a business when you've never set foot in its premises?

If you seriously want a particular job you'll do your homework *before* you fill in an application or go to an interview. You'll find out everything you can about the company you're applying to, what it does, what it is like to work for, its strengths and weaknesses. After you've got the job you want, you'll use your knowledge of the business to improve your contribution to it and to play your part in the organisation to the full.

In this chapter we'll show you what to look for to understand a business and how to go about getting the information you need. But first we'll look at some general principles that apply to every company regardless of what it does.

How does the company work?

If you've never worked before, you can be forgiven for thinking that most companies are the same. They have employees and managers who tell the workers what to do; they make money for their owners or shareholders; they have customers to whom they provide a product or service.

In essence all that is true but in reality organisations vary a lot. They have different management structures; they may not make money for owners/shareholders but plough their profits into the community; they will have customers – but these will come from both outside and inside the business.

Let's look at an example – British Gas.

You may think that British Gas is an independent organisation that provides gas and electricity to customers. In fact all the following points apply to the company:

- British Gas is part of the Centrica Group, a large organisation in the energy industry that also has other interests.
- The company provides gas and electricity to both domestic and industrial/commercial customers. It also offers a range of home services such as insurance, repairs and home-care products.
- It employs almost 30,000 people in a wide range of jobs from engineering through to marketing and legal services. In fact, in an organisation of this size there are few jobs that you *won't* find an opportunity to explore!
- The company has offices and bases all over the country.

What does the company aim to do?

Most large organisations – and many small ones – have what is known as a mission statement. This is a short statement that summarises its aims and values – what it wants to do and how it intends to achieve this. Let's look at British Gas again. The company website states the following:

> Our vision for British Gas is simple; by deepening our relationships with our customers through value for money, better service and innovation, we aim to be the number one choice for energy and services today, as well as in the smarter homes and businesses of tomorrow.
>
> Source: www.britishgasjobs.co.uk/about-us/the-company.

The company has defined three values that sum up the way it wants to operate.

Do what's right

We care about doing what's right for our customers, for each other and our business.
We use our heads and our hearts to make fair decisions and we're not afraid to hold ourselves to account.

Love simplicity

We keep things simple and focus on what really matters.

We're passionate about making it easy.

Be extraordinary together

We do bigger and better things when we work together.

We use our unique mix of people and skills to deliver great service.

We recently completed a business-wide review to highlight what we need
to focus on to reach our full potential.

Source: www.britishgasjobs.co.uk/about-us/values-and-strategic-priorities.

So how is this information relevant to you if you're thinking about applying
for a job, traineeship or apprenticeship with the organisation?

The mission statement and values actually tell you a lot about what the
company wants to achieve and hence what sort of employees it is looking
for. They tell us that the company:

- is customer-focused and wants employees who will be
  responsive to customers
- wants employees who are willing to be held to account for
  what they do, not to shirk responsibility
- is innovative and will be looking for staff who have ideas and can
  keep the business at the forefront of the energy industry
- wants team players, people who are willing to work together and
  contribute rather than try to go it alone.

This information will help you to identify if this is your sort of employer. If
you're a loner who hates teamwork and is not good at taking responsibility
for your own mistakes, then British Gas is probably not for you. Knowing
what the company is looking for will enable you to focus on your strengths
that fit with their culture; you can prepare evidence of ways in which you
have proved that you can be innovative or been a good team player.

Who are the customers?

When you go to work, you'll find that the word 'customers' has a whole new meaning. It doesn't just refer to the obvious clients but to a whole range of people both outside and inside an organisation. As an employee, your customers will be anyone who requires something from you or is a stakeholder in the business.

All organisations have both internal and external customers.

- An internal customer is anyone who is connected with the organisation – employees, managers, board members, shareholders.
- An external customer is someone you deal with who is not part of the organisation – the people that we generally call our clients or customers. They are the people who buy a service or product.

Going back to the example we've been using, British Gas, imagine that you get a job in the company's human-resources department. Your job will entail keeping both your internal and external customers happy. Here are some examples of your internal customers.

- The company staff that you look after and help with employment issues.
- Line managers who need your help in recruiting more staff.
- Senior management who rely on you to carry out the company's long-term plans relating to human resources.
- Shareholders who want the company to make a profit. You may never meet them, but they are relying on you to contribute to the success of the company so that it makes money and stays in business.

Here are some examples of your external customers.

- Job applicants – you need to look after them so that they get a good introduction to the company. If a potential new recruit rings up the HR department with a query about their forthcoming interview and gets an off-hand, abrupt response, how will they feel about the company and the people that work there? It could be very off-putting.
- People who supply HR with goods or services. Maybe your HR department uses external recruitment agencies sometimes to find specialist staff. If your manner is not helpful, will that recruitment agency always do its best for you? Or will the word go round that you're not a nice person to deal with?

Where do you fit into the organisation?

Another area that you should be clear about is how the job you want fits in with the rest of the business. Say you get a job as a customer assistant in a supermarket. The minute you start work, you'll become part of a team. You will probably be supervised by more senior customer assistants and team leaders, who in turn are supervised by an assistant manager who reports to the store manager. The store manager may be answerable to the area manager, who looks after a number of supermarkets in a specific location; the area managers will report to the regional managers ... And overseeing the work of this large team are the directors who are responsible for the organisation's policy and making sure that it thrives in the future so that shareholders will continue to invest.

All these team leaders and managers that you work with have targets to achieve and your job is to help them succeed in doing this by being willing to turn a hand to a range of tasks and acting as a brand ambassador so the supermarket's customers will always be happy with the service they receive and continue visiting your store.

Do your research

Before you apply for a job, find out all you can about it. Research has never been easier because most companies have an internet presence. Many have dedicated sections on their websites specifically for job seekers like yourselves who are just starting their careers. These will give you lots of information that will help you prepare your application and for interview.

Use this template to get you started. When you come across a company that you're interested in working for, find out the following information. Use the internet, talk to people, Google the company and see what others say about it.

Company's name and core business	
What the company says it wants to achieve (mission statement)	
Job/department I'm applying for	
What work does this involve?	
Who will I report to?	
Who will my external customers be?	
Who will my internal customers be?	

Look at Claire's experience.

When I was sixteen, I decided to look for an apprenticeship as an electrician. I didn't want to go to university and build up a load of debt and I was keen to get hands-on experience rather than learn a lot of theory.

I looked at three organisations before I put in my applications and found out as much about them as I could. The information that was most valuable was about the apprenticeship training – how it was structured, how much time I'd spend at college, what type of work the company focused on, etc. From their websites, I found out which of them had trained female electricians before and what jobs the apprentices got after they qualified. Other useful information was about promotion structures; that showed me what opportunities the companies offered, how many vacancies they had and where they were located.

Once I started researching, I got really into it and looked at all sorts of documents like company reports and feedback from customers. One of the companies did a lot of work in the local community for charity, which I liked. Another had a policy called 'lifelong learning' where it encouraged staff to keep training and getting more qualifications.

I applied to two of the organisations because I liked the way they presented themselves and their attitude towards their staff. Having some background knowledge gave me confidence when I was interviewed and I think I got some brownie points for having done some homework. I got the apprenticeship I wanted and it's working out really well.

To sum it all up ...

- Learn all you can about organisations you are interested in before you apply to them. Your knowledge will impress potential employers.
- Find out what the organisation aims to do by looking for a mission statement or a summary of its values and work.
- When you're working, be aware of the company structure. Your own work will impact on many other people's work.
- Always be aware of your 'customers', both outside and inside the business.

11 Write your own profile

You've completed a lot of work as you read this book and we hope it's opened your eyes to what you are really capable of. You have many skills that you've developed through your education, domestic and social life. Many of these can be put to use when you start your career.

In this chapter, you're going to review what you've achieved. We'll ask you to look at the different skills areas that we've focused on and to identify:

  ◾ what you're good at
  ◾ what you need to improve on.

You will then prepare a skills profile that identifies what you can already do and, most importantly, gives evidence of your skills. You can use this as a basis for job or higher-education applications and refer to it before interviews. When you're feeling a bit unsure of your future, it will give you confidence by providing a permanent record of the skills you already possess.

We'll also ask you to prepare an action plan for the future so that you can see how to improve your skills base.

Skills review

Draw up some charts like the ones on the next few pages on a separate piece of paper. These will help you to review the skills that you currently have and those that you need to improve.

You need to create two types of chart – one for your strengths, one for your weaknesses. For your strengths, in the first column select specific skills in which you feel that you are already competent. In the second column make a note of something that you've done that proves you have this skill.

For your weaknesses, list skills that you feel less confident about in the left-hand column. In the second column make a note of why you think you're weak in this area.

We've included some examples to get you started.

Communication skills

(e.g. written communications, listening, speaking on the telephone, speaking to groups of people, contributing to meetings, giving instructions, etc.)

Strengths

Areas that I excel in	This is evidenced by
Communicate well on the telephone.	Persuaded local businesses to advertise in our school yearbook.

Weaknesses

Areas that I need to improve	This is evidenced by
Speaking in public.	I've only done this once and was too nervous to get my message across clearly.

Teamworking skills

(e.g. collaborating with others, organising a team, learning new skills from other team members, chairing a meeting, etc.)

Strengths

Areas that I excel in	This is evidenced by
Getting people to work together as a team.	I got 20 people to work together to raise funds for charity by producing a Comic Relief joke book.

Weaknesses

Areas that I need to improve	This is evidenced by
I tend to boss other people about.	Complaints from my friends when they've worked with me!

Problem-solving skills

(e.g. collecting and analysing data, consulting other people, analysing problems, using problem-solving tools, etc.)

Strengths

Areas that I excel in	This is evidenced by
Research – finding things out in libraries and on the internet.	The history of art project that I completed as part of my A level course. This involved original research about local artists.

Weaknesses

Areas that I need to improve	This is evidenced by
Understanding numerical data.	I avoid using this type of information even when I know it would be relevant.

Using numbers

(e.g. calculations using electronic equipment, mental arithmetic, calculating weights, measures and space, percentages and fractions, etc.)

Strengths

Areas that I excel in	This is evidenced by
Estimating amounts of material needed to complete projects.	I helped my parents to calculate what materials they would need to redesign and landscape their garden. There was no significant over-purchase of materials.

Weaknesses

Areas that I need to improve	This is evidenced by
Preparing simple accounts.	My poor performance in preparing the final profit and loss account for the Comic Relief joke book.

ICT

(e.g. using word-processing packages, spreadsheets, email, presentation software, etc.)

Strengths

Areas that I excel in	This is evidenced by
Word processing.	The way that I present my coursework.

Weaknesses

Areas that I need to improve	This is evidenced by
Using a database.	I've never done this though I know it would be useful for storing information about friends and family.

Skills profile

Using the information that you've identified in the previous section, you can now write your own skills profile. Do this on a separate piece of paper and remember to keep it for future reference.

Imagine that you're applying for a job and you want to highlight your skills in your CV or a covering letter. Write a brief paragraph that describes what you can do in each of the following skills areas and provide evidence to support your claims.

This is one occasion in your life when you don't need to be too modest. We're not suggesting that you appear unbearably conceited – but you do need to state clearly what you are capable of doing. Don't be embarrassed when you list your achievements; you're not boasting. But do be honest. If you lie about, or over-exaggerate, your achievements you may be found out.

Action plan

As you prepared your skills review and identified your existing skills and competences, you'll have recognised areas where you want to improve or gain more experience. These will form the basis for an action plan that sets out what you hope to achieve in the future and how you'll go about it.

Before you start, a few words about action planning. It's important that you're realistic about what you want to achieve and that you don't try to do too much at once. Saying 'I want to improve my communication skills' is of no practical use because it's a general statement and doesn't suggest a process that you can follow. Worse still, you may not even be sure what you mean by 'improving your communication skills'.

What you need to do is to develop a logical set of stages that will help you to target a specific skills area that you want to improve.

■ Start by identifying the general area that you're planning to focus on first. Choose one area (e.g. IT skills, problem-solving skills, communication skills, etc.). If you try to address too many skills gaps at once, you'll feel defeated before you start.

■ Now narrow down the skills area that you've chosen to one particular concern. For example, if you've identified verbal-communication skills as an area for improvement, think about which part of your communication skills causes you most concern. Is it your listening skills? Your ability to give instructions? Making presentations or public speaking? Focus on something specific.

■ Now narrow this focus again. Why is this skill important to your work? How will improving this skill make your working life more productive and easier? So, for example, if you've decided that you want to improve your presentation skills, think about when you use this skill and what you use it for. Being clear about why you're working to improve a particular skill is a powerful motivator.

■ Break down the components of the skill that you want to improve. If it is your presentation skills, you can identify a number of activities that contribute to making a presentation: using IT; speaking to an audience; controlling your nervousness; preparing a talk; preparing handouts; getting feedback from your audience, etc.

■ Now that you have a clearer idea of what you want to achieve, you can set some specific objectives. Again, limit these to one or two and don't try to do too much at once. Here's an example related to presentation skills: 'My objective is to use PowerPoint to make a presentation to my team.'

■ To make life easier, make your objectives SMART (specific, measurable, achievable, relevant and time-bound). This gives a clear picture of what you want to achieve, how you will achieve it, what help you'll need and when you hope to have completed your skills improvement.

SMART objectives

To make objectives more achievable, it helps to make them SMART.

Specific: *your objective should be clearly defined (e.g. I want to use PowerPoint to make a presentation).*

Measurable: *you should have a definite output for your objective to show that you've achieved it (e.g. the presentation that has been made using PowerPoint).*

Achievable: *the objective should be something that you know you are capable of achieving (e.g. you would find it hard to master PowerPoint if you were a complete novice in using computers).*

Relevant: *the objective should have a direct link to something you really need to or want to do for work (e.g. mastering PowerPoint will make it easier to make presentations).*

Time-bound: *there should be a date by which you'll have achieved your objective (e.g. I plan to master PowerPoint within six weeks).*

Here's an example.

My objective	How I'll do this	Help/resources needed	How I'll know I've achieved it	Completed by
To use PowerPoint to make a presentation	1. Take a course at local learning centre 2. Practise at home in my own time	1. Training course 2. PowerPoint instruction book/ worksheets/ YouTube 3. Interactive websites	When I can prepare a presentation with 12 slides using different layouts and designs	Six weeks from now

This is a very simple example, but it gives you some idea of how the process works. Rather than vaguely saying, 'I really need to learn to use presentation software,' this action plan breaks down the work involved and helps you to get started.

Now try the staged approach yourself.

1. The skills area I want to improve is …
2. I specifically want to improve …
3. This will help me because …
4. The particular aspect of (2) that I am going to work on first is …
5. My objective is ..:

Fill in a chart like the one on the next page to show how you will achieve this objective.

My objective	How I'll do this	Help/resources needed	How I'll know I've achieved it	Completed by

To make sure that you fulfil your objective, report your progress to someone else. This could be a manager, a colleague or a friend. Show them your action plan and set dates (every two weeks would be good) when you will get together to discuss your progress. You should also arrange a meeting with them for the date when you plan to complete your objective; this gives you something to work towards and a 'signing-off' point.

You can use this action-plan template as many times as you like as you address different skills areas that you want to improve.

And finally …

Leaving school or college and starting work can be a daunting experience. Yes, it's exciting and it's great to be trying something new, but it can also be challenging. Don't be surprised if at first you sometimes feel confused or frightened. Everybody does, it's just that some of us are better at hiding our nervousness.

What Employers Want

The thrust of this book has been to explore some of the skills that will make you employable and to show you that you already possess many of these skills.

Employers are not some alien race. Cut through the hype and the corporate mission statements and the jargon and you'll see that most of them are ordinary people who simply want their businesses to succeed.

To achieve that goal, they need staff who can make an effective contribution. Specifically, they need recruits who can:

- fit into the organisation
- pull their weight
- prove their reliability.

In this book we've also highlighted some specific skills that employers require:

- the ability to communicate easily and effectively with other people
- the ability to work and interact with other people
- the ability to solve problems and make decisions when required
- proficiency in using words, numbers and ICT
- a commitment to improving performance – both the company's and the employee's own.

You will have already demonstrated that you can do these things at school and college.

- You've communicated with your teachers, friends, people younger than yourself and people in authority.
- You've worked with other people in class, in extra-curricular activities, such as team sports, and with your friends.

- You've regularly solved problems and made decisions, ranging from minor ones about your daily routine to major ones about what to study.
- You use words, numbers and ICT on a regular basis both at school/college and in the outside world.
- You've shown a commitment to getting through your school career and gaining qualifications.
- You've also shown a commitment to developing your career by reading this book!

We hope you now recognise your achievements more clearly and how these could be relevant to an employer. This will help you to present yourself in the best light when you apply for a job, and to become a valued member of staff when you get that job.

A willingness to learn, a positive attitude and respect for other people will get you a long way in your new career. Treat others as you want to be treated and believe in yourself. By reading this book you should have discovered just how much you're capable of.

Good luck!

12 Further information

Need some more advice?

The last few years have not been easy for young people joining the job market. News reports are full of doom and gloom about redundancies, fewer vacancies, cuts in training opportunities and over-subscribed university and college places.

Before this puts you in a panic and you decide that entering the employment market isn't worth the effort, take a step back. Remember that the media has a tendency to focus on the bad news rather than the good. Yes, these are difficult times – but they are nothing new. We've weathered recessions and high unemployment in the past and we'll survive them in the future. And, according to a House of Common Briefing Paper published in August 2016, 626,000 young people aged 16–24 were unemployed in April–June 2016, down 5,000 from the previous quarter and down 105,000 compared to a year ago so, at least for the time being, more young people are finding work.

There is now more help out there for young people who are going into employment than there has ever been. Advice centres, careers experts, trainers, books, websites and telephone helplines have become more accessible, their advice is free and they really can help you.

If you're still in education, either at school or college/university, you should have access to careers advice. This will often include guidance on skills development and will almost certainly give you practical help in preparing your CV so that you can showcase your abilities to the best effect.

Here is a list of some information sources that you might like to check out. Most of them are web-based so they are available to everyone regardless of where they live.

National Careers Service (England)

nationalcareersservice.direct.gov.uk provides information, advice and guidance across England to help you make decisions on learning, training and work opportunities. The organisation's website aims to:

- help you with careers decisions and planning
- support you in reviewing your skills and abilities and develop new goals
- motivate you to implement your plan of action
- enable you to make the best use of high-quality career related tools.

There is also valuable information about bursaries and salaries related to both work and training schemes like apprenticeships.

My World of Work

www.myworldofwork.co.uk offers a similar service in Scotland. It can help you:

- discover careers that match your skills, interests, education and experience
- research jobs, industries and Modern Apprenticeships that might suit you
- find practical tools and advice to help you get the job you want
- find vacancies in your local area.

The website has a host of tools to help you find information about appropriate courses, volunteering, funding, CVs, interviews and job vacancies.

Careers Wales

www.careerswales.com gives bilingual (Welsh and English) advice for anyone looking for a job at any age. It has useful sections on apprenticeships, traineeships and Job Growth Wales opportunities, as well as an excellent Skills Gateway section that will help you with job applications.

Careers Service Northern Ireland

www.nidirect.gov.uk/ has an equally good resource that offers help to anyone age 13 or over onwards who is interested in looking at careers opportunities and skills development. The skills sections offer lots of resources and contacts if you're looking for courses to improve your functional skills.

Apprenticeships

www.gov.uk/topic/further-education-skills/apprenticeships. Apprentice-ships are a huge growth area to which the government has pledged financial assistance. In 2014–15 there was an increase of 115% in the number of higher apprenticeship starts compared with the previous year – and there are plans to double the amount of investment in schemes by 2020. Apprenticeships have increased in popularity as more people have recognised the value of learning while working – and like the idea of earning money while they learn their job. Also, apprenticeships are now available in many different disciplines; they cover 1,200 job roles in a range of industries, from engineering to financial advice, veterinary nursing to accountancy.

Career Connect

www.careerconnect.org.uk is a charity that provides independent careers advice that bridges the gap between learning and employment. It provides a wide range of career-management services, some funded by Local Authorities and schools and colleges in local areas.

Skillswise

www.bbc.co.uk/skillswise is a BBC website that will help you to improve your literacy and numeracy skills. It provides hundreds of worksheets and interactive pages and it's fun to use.

Glossary

We've included a brief glossary of some of the terms that have been used in this book.

Attitude

Your attitude in the context of this book is the way that you feel and think about work. Employers want recruits who are positive about working, who genuinely want a career and have a 'can do' attitude. These recruits will rise to challenges and also be willing to contribute to the success of the company. If you have a positive attitude and are excited about the prospect of starting work, you are already ahead in the employment stakes.

Behaviours

Behaviours are the ways that you act. Again, employers look for people who display positive behaviours that show they are engaged with their work such as punctuality, thoroughness in completing tasks, friendliness towards other staff, etc.

Employability skills

The Confederation of British Industry defines employability skills as:

> A set of attributes, skills and knowledge that all labour market participants should possess to ensure they have the capability of being effective in the workplace – to the benefit of themselves, their employer and the wider economy.

Evidence

We talk a lot in this book about 'providing evidence' of your skills. Essentially, this means being able to prove that you can do what you say you can do. Anyone can claim to have excellent communication skills but an employer wants to know that these claims can be fulfilled and will look for information about times when you've communicated effectively at work.

What Employers Want

Functional skills
These are practical skills that you can apply to any job, particularly using numbers, language and IT effectively.

Mission statement
This is a short statement that summarises an organisation's aims and values. It will help you to understand what sort of business this is and what it wants to do for its customers.

Personal skills
These skills used to be described as 'soft' skills and relate to aspects of your character rather than describing practical things that you can do. Examples would be working with other people in teams and communicating effectively.

Skills
These are things you can do (or will learn to do). See the definitions for *employability*, *functional* and *personal skills*.